THE HEALTHY TEEN COOKBOOK

For permission requests, please contact the publisher at:

Mango Publishing Group
2850 Douglas Road, 3rd Floor
Coral Gables, FL 33134 U.S.A.
info@mango.bz

For special orders, quantity sales, course adoptions and corporate sales, please email the publisher at sales@mango.bz. For trade and wholesale sales, please contact Ingram Publisher Services at customer.service@ingramcontent.com or +1.800.509.4887.

The Healthy Teen Cookbook: Around the World in 80 Fantastic Recipes

Library of Congress Cataloging
ISBN: (hardcover) 978-1-63353-665-4, (e-book) 978-1-63353-666-1
Library of Congress Control Number: 2017915645
BISAC category code: YAN014000 YOUNG ADULT NONFICTION / Cooking & Food

Printed in the United States of America

THE HEALTHY TEEN COOKBOOK

Around the World in
80 Fantastic Recipes

REMMI SMITH

To my family, friends, and mentors—thank you for endless support and inspiration.

To all the aspiring cooks and chefs around the world, cooking is both a skill and an art—add your own flair in the kitchen and you will be just fine!

CONTENTS

CONTINENT OF EUROPE

CONTINENT OF AFRICA

CONTINENT OF ASIA

CONTINENT OF AUSTRALIA

CONTINENT OF ANTARCTICA

ACKNOWLEDGMENTS

ABOUT THE CHEF

COOKBOOK MASTER INTRODUCTION

Hi!

First, thank YOU so much for picking up this cookbook and trying it out! I'm Remmi Smith, author of the cookbook you hold in your hands, as well as another called *Global Cooking for Kids*. Before you get into the really good stuff, I figure I should tell you a little bit about myself. I am seventeen years old, and I love food. I love to cook and I love to eat, but most importantly, I love to share my love of food with others! I began in the kitchen at the tender age of four years old. Granted, back then, I was doing more eating than I was cooking. But soon my mom assigned me easy tasks like washing fruits and vegetables or mixing salads. (I took these assignments very seriously at four years old; you wouldn't have spotted a speck of dirt on any produce that passed through my sink.) Soon, I became hooked on being in the kitchen, and I spent most of my early childhood there. My mom began to teach me basic cooking skills and I ran with them. By the time I was seven years old, I could make a full meal on my own. (It was meatloaf, which is not exactly spectacular, but a win is a win.) Flash forward a whole decade—boy, that makes me feel old—and I have now had two cooking shows, two cookbooks published, and my own salad dressing line, with no slowdown in sight. Now, enough about me, let's focus on the food.

While writing this cookbook, I had three main goals in mind: (1) to make cooking and eating as healthy and fun as possible; (2) to ensure that teens will be able to do it; and (3) to take you on a global adventure! Hopefully, by the end of reading this cookbook and making these dishes, I will have succeeded in these goals, and you'll be able to show off your fancy, new kitchen skills.

Cooking is not only an important life skill but an experience, which is why I want to make this book a journey for you (both literally and figuratively). After traversing a mere eighty recipes, you will have traveled through thirty-nine countries, while exploring the native cuisine of each, their cultural traditions, and their holidays! You will take a taste of each country while traipsing across all seven continents. You will be able to explore the rich history behind many of these nations, and you'll discover the origins of dishes that you may not have known about before.

The world is your oyster (I think that is some kind of food wordplay), or rather, the world is your kitchen (that fits much better)! Try your hand at Norwegian, South African, or Polish cuisine! This book gives you the chance to travel the globe through food and culture. You can even learn about the types of food prepared in Antarctica! (We asked some penguins about their food preferences.*) Also, after reading this book, not only will you have a head full of random facts about various countries and cuisines, but you can also tell your friends that you have traveled the world without the need for a passport! I hope you enjoy this cookbook and the food you will make using it. *Bon Voyage!*

Hugs and Veggies,

Remmi

---

*Of course, I am only kidding, we conferred with humans.

REMMI'S 10 TIPS TO BECOMING A GREAT COOK

1. **FOLLOW THE RULES**

   Always ensure kitchen safety and kitchen cleanliness.

2. **BE ORGANIZED**

   Cut and measure all ingredients before you start cooking.

3. **FOLLOW THE RECIPE**

   (As a beginner cook.)

4. **CLEAN UP**

   It's the least fun, but necessary, part of cooking.

5. **READ ABOUT FOOD**

   Especially a variety of recipes and food history.

6. **BE INSPIRED**

   Try creating your own recipes!

7. **USE LOTS OF FRUITS AND VEGGIES**

   Color makes each dish beautiful.

8. **COOK HEALTHY**

   There are many healthy substitutions available.

9. **PRESENTATION IS INCREDIBLY IMPORTANT**

   Remember the saying, "we eat with our eyes."

10. **HAVE FUN!**

    You will; I promise!

ABOUT THE RECIPES

When selecting these recipes, I tried to pick popular dishes and ingredients that are readily available and frequently served in their respective countries. I was inspired to experiment with many dishes, and I read various recipes of the same dish before I began cooking. My preferences to customizing recipes are to use a lot of vegetables (fortunately, there is only one vegetable that I am not crazy about), add natural sweetness through the use of fruits (I've got a sweet spot for natural sweets), go light on spices (which makes it easier for kids to try new foods), substitute low-fat ingredients (making it healthier), include easy-to-follow steps (making it easier for kids to tackle), present some fun facts or history (which makes food interesting), and present the dish beautifully. I also try to select economical foods so that my recipes are budget-friendly, too!

CONTINENT OF NORTH AMERICA

"Real food doesn't have ingredients. Real food is ingredients."
—**Jamie Oliver**

North America has the fourth largest population among the continents and has the third largest land mass. Lake Superior is the largest freshwater lake in the world. Twenty-three countries make up North America. The United States has the largest population, Canada has the largest land mass, and Mexico City is the most populated city. This continent also has the largest island, Greenland. Let's begin our travels around the world with the northernmost country we'll be visiting on this continent.

Canada is the second largest nation in the world, right after Russia. Over half of Canada's residents have college degrees, making it the world's most educated country. Yonge Street, the longest street in the world, starts at Lake Ontario, and runs to the Minnesota border, a distance of about 2,000 km! Approximately 77 percent of the world's maple syrup comes from Canada.

Tourtière is a meat pie that originated in the province of Québec. This French-Canadian dish is often prepared with a combination of two or sometimes three meats, such as beef, pork, veal, chicken, or wild game like rabbit. The dish is primarily meat prepared with some kind of binder such as potatoes, oats, or breadcrumbs. Spices like cinnamon and allspice are in most, if not all, tourtière recipes. In French-Canadian homes, this dish is a must during the Christmas and New Year's holidays.

TOURTIÈRE WITH SWEET AND SPICY KETCHUP

INGREDIENTS:

2 Tbsp. olive oil

1 cup onion (medium dice)

½ cup celery (small dice)

1½ lb. ground chuck (lean)

½ cup carrots (medium dice)

1 large Yukon Gold potato (unpeeled)

1 cup beef broth

½ tsp. cinnamon

¼ tsp. allspice

Salt and pepper to taste

2 Tbsp. flour

2 Tbsp. fresh parsley (sliced)

1 Tbsp. sage (finely chopped)

1 recipe double crust pie crust (prepared)

1 egg (white only)

1 Tbsp. water

½ cup ketchup

1 tsp. brown sugar

1 tsp. Sriracha

DIRECTIONS:

Preheat oven to 350 degrees. Prepare all of the ingredients as directed. In medium pan, heat the olive oil and add the onion, celery, and ground beef. Sauté until the meat is no longer pink. Drain if there is excess grease. Add the carrots, potato, broth, allspice, and cinnamon, and salt and pepper to taste. Bring to a boil and then turn down the heat. Cook until the potatoes are just crisp but tender. Additional broth or water may be needed to keep mixture moist while cooking. Add flour and stir until combined. Add parsley and sage and mix well. When cooking is finished, cool the mixture completely before putting the pie together.

Prepare the pie pan by lining it with the crust and then fill with the beef mixture. Finish the pie by adding the pastry top and crimping the edges to seal the pie. Cut 3 or 4 slits to allow for the steam to escape. Mix the water with the egg white and brush the top of the pie with the resulting egg wash. Place in the oven for 45 minutes or until the crust is golden brown. Let the pie rest for 15 minutes before serving. While the pie is cooking, in a small bowl combine the ketchup, sugar, and Sriracha. Heat the ketchup blend the in microwave before serving. Serve the ketchup with the pie as a condiment.

REMMI NOTES: Cottage pie, which is another meat pie, is one of my all-time favorites, but when I finally settled on my personal version of the tourtière, it became my favorite! No matter what, this pie makes for a beautiful presentation. I also added veggies to make it healthier. Serve the dish with the spicy ketchup for a bolder flavor. I have given you an easy recipe, but there are recipes you can use to make ketchup from scratch, which is for sure superior to this quick version. Serve the pie with a salad for a complete meal. Hope you enjoy this!

From Canada, if you go south and skip over the entire United States, you will land here. Mexico is the fourteenth largest country in the world. *Fútbol* is the most popular sport, but it is what is called "soccer" in the United States. One of their most well-known holidays is *El Día de Los Muertos*, which means "the Day of the Dead"; it is celebrated from October 31st to November 1st. On those two nights, many go to cemeteries to set up altars bearing photos of their kin who have passed. They bring their loved ones' favorite foods, burn candles, and play games with the children. The true spirit of the holiday is the prayers and remembrances of family members and friends who have died. A favorite holiday dish is *pan de muerto*, translating to "Bread of the Dead." It is a type of sweet roll, usually with bone-shaped decorations.

Corn, beans, rice, and tomatoes are Mexican staples found in many of their dishes. Jícama is a root vegetable that originated in Mexico; it is almost always served raw, and is usually served with a salad like this one. I substituted apple for the jícama, as they are often hard to find; the apple brings a sweeter profile to the salad. Mexican cuisine is full of flavor and spices and includes a lot of heat, meaning spiciness. Albondigas, which was brought to Mexico by the Spanish conquistadors, is the embodiment of Mexican comfort food. It is a warm broth served with miniature meatballs, creating the perfect balance of flavors. You can choose to add extra spice. It often includes many fresh vegetables—whatever is in season works! Serve albondigas along with this chopped salad for a healthy take on Mexican cuisine.

MEXICAN CHOPPED SALAD

Prep time: 15 minutes • Cook time: 5 minutes

INGREDIENTS:

3 cup romaine lettuce (1" dice)

1 cup green apple (peeled, ½" dice)

1 cup cherry tomatoes (sliced in half)

¾ cup corn (fresh/grilled preferred)

¾ cup black beans (rinsed and drained)

1 cup cucumber (½" dice)

2 green onions (sliced thin)

⅓ cup oil

⅓ cup lime juice

¼ tsp. red pepper

Salt and pepper to taste

Cilantro (garnish)

DIRECTIONS:

Prepare all of the ingredients as directed. In a medium bowl, add all salad ingredients. In a small bowl, mix the oil, lime juice, red pepper, and salt and pepper. When ready to serve, toss the salad with the desired amount of dressing and garnish with cilantro.

REMMI NOTES: I think this chopped salad is one of the most easily prepared dishes that contains the most robust flavor—the dressing highlights each ingredient and brings the note of freshness that every salad needs!

ALBONDIGAS SOUP (MEATBALL SOUP)

INGREDIENTS:

1 lb. ground beef (lean)

1/3 cup raw white rice

2 Tbsp. parsley (chopped)

2 Tbsp. cilantro (chopped)

½ tsp. garlic powder

1 egg

1 Tbsp. olive oil

1 cup onion (medium dice)

1 Anaheim green chile (medium dice)

2 garlic cloves (minced)

32 oz. chicken broth (low fat)

3 Roma tomatoes (large dice)

2 carrots (sliced ½" rounds)

2 celery stalks (sliced)

1 large potato (large dice)

1 cup tomato sauce

Salt and pepper to taste

1 cup peas

½ cup cilantro (garnish)

2 limes (sliced for garnish)

½ cup salsa (garnish)

DIRECTIONS:

Mix the first 6 ingredients in medium bowl. Shape the meat mixture into 1½" meatballs, packed tightly, and set aside. In a large pot, over medium heat sauté the onions, garlic, and chiles in the olive oil until tender. To the pot, add broth and bring to a boil. Add the tomatoes, carrots, celery potatoes, tomato sauce, and salt and pepper. Bring to a boil and gently add the meatballs to the soup. Turn the heat to medium-low and simmer for 30 minutes or until the meatballs are cooked and vegetables are tender. Add the peas and cook for 2 minutes. Garnish with cilantro, limes, and salsa on the side. Serve with warm tortillas.

REMMI NOTES: This is a very popular soup in Mexico and is often described as "Mexican Soul Food." I became interested in this dish because of the meatballs! Who doesn't like meatballs?! There are a lot of different recipes for this famous dish; I created my recipe with some of my favorite foods, like carrots!

From Mexico, we will be journeying deeper into Central America, the southernmost portion of the North American continent. Honduras is the second largest country in Central America. The country has extensive coastal areas bordering the Pacific Ocean and the Caribbean Sea. The country is rich in minerals, tropical fruits, and coffee—some major Honduran exports.

I read about the most interesting Honduran phenomenon—the annual *Lluvia de Peces*, or "rain of fish," that occurs in the small town of Yoro. After the occurrence, a festive celebration takes place. This natural event has been happening for the past one hundred years, and in recent years, it has been happening twice a year. In the midst of a strong storm, fish that are not indigenous to the area rain from the sky. After the storm, the streets are filled with live fish. There are several theories about it, ranging from the scientific to the possibility that it's a miracle and cannot be scientifically explained. Research more about this interesting phenomenon and decide for yourself what you believe is happening. https://scholar.google.com/

The Honduran Baleada is a traditional fare for Hondurans. It is a flour tortilla filled with ingredients such as meats, vegetables, and eggs. A form of this dish can be served at breakfast, lunch, or dinner. For breakfast, it can simply consist of refried beans served with "mantequilla crema," which has a similar taste and texture to sour cream. The recipe for my Baleada combines meat, beans, eggs, and sour cream...yes—I combined all my favorite ingredients!

HONDURAN BALEADAS

INGREDIENTS:

1 Tbsp. olive oil

1½ lb. sirloin or beef round (sliced in 1"
pieces)

2 garlic cloves (sliced)

1 cup onion (medium dice)

2 poblano peppers (medium dice)

1 Tbsp. jalapeño pepper (diced)

28 oz. diced tomatoes

½ to ¾ cup vegetable stock

½ tsp. cumin

¼ tsp. oregano

2 Tbsp. cornstarch (mixed with 1 Tbsp.
water)

1-14 oz. can pinto beans (rinsed/drained)

4 eggs (hard-boiled and sliced)

8 small flour tortillas or 4 large flour
tortillas (see Remmi Notes below)

Sour cream (low fat or nonfat)

DIRECTIONS:

In a medium pan, add the olive oil, meat, onion, garlic, and peppers, and sauté until meat is browned. Add the tomatoes, vegetable stock, cumin, and oregano. Bring to a boil, then add the cornstarch/water mixture and stir. Turn the heat to low and cover pan with a lid; let simmer for 30 minutes.

To serve, place 2 Tbsp. of pinto beans on one half of the flour tortilla. Spoon ⅓ to ½ cup of meat mixture over the beans. Place a spoonful of egg slices on top of meat. Fold the top half over the meat mixture. Dip Baleadas in sour cream and enjoy!

REMMI NOTES: The Baleada is often referred to as "The Honduran Burrito." There are many different ingredients you can use to make Baleadas…research different recipes. This dish is so delicious!!! I also make homemade flour tortillas, which are not difficult to make, and the fresh taste is worth it!

Moving east of Central America we travel over the Caribbean Sea to the Greater Antilles, a group of large islands, one of which is Cuba. Known officially as the Republic of Cuba, this island nation is located in the Caribbean Sea. Cuba is rich in Spanish history, as well as many cultural influences from Africa. Sugar is its largest crop. Havana is the capital of Cuba and has one of the finest natural harbors found anywhere. Dancing is very important to Cubans; the Bolero, Cha Cha, and Mambo originated there. The popular game of "Monopoly" is banned in the country, but the game of "Dominos" is a favorite pastime. Cuba has one of the highest literacy rates in the world at 99.8 percent.

Cuban cuisine is a fusion of Spanish and African influences. The cuisine is similar to that of Puerto Rico. I was looking for something different to try and fell in love with Picadillo. This dish reminds me of sloppy joes, and I think any teen will fall for this recipe. There are many versions of this dish. It is like a beef hash with a tomato base and some unusual ingredients like olives, capers, and raisins. I am not a caper lover, so you won't find that in my recipe. I also decreased the amount of olives and raisins. Maybe I just wanted to make my sloppy joe recipe!

PICADILLO

INGREDIENTS:

2 Tbsp. olive oil

1 cup onion

1 cup green bell pepper (medium dice)

2 garlic cloves (crushed)

Crushed red pepper (to taste)

1½ tsp. cumin

½ tsp. cinnamon

¼ tsp. nutmeg

1½ lb. ground beef (lean)

4 oz. tomatoes (diced)

8 oz. tomato sauce

Salt and pepper to taste

¼ cup raisins

⅓ cup pimento olives (large dice)

Flour tortillas (4 to 6)

2 cups leaf lettuce (sliced in ½" strips)

DIRECTIONS:

Prepare all of the ingredients as directed. In a medium saucepan, add the oil and heat on medium. Add the onion, pepper, and garlic. Sauté for 2 minutes. Add red pepper, cumin, cinnamon, nutmeg, and ground beef to the same pan. Sauté the meat until no longer pink. Add the tomatoes and sauce to the pan and simmer for 15 minutes. Stir in the raisins and olives and heat through. Serve with flour tortillas and lettuce.

REMMI NOTES: Some recipes add potatoes to this dish as a base. The dish is often served with rice and beans, the national mainstay dish. I was interested in something different, so I tried making it with flour tortillas and loved it. Serve this dish with a healthy version of "Fried Plantains" using coconut oil for a complete meal.

On our next journey we hop across the Windward Passage just south of Cuba to Haiti, which is part of the island of Hispaniola. Haiti is the most mountainous nation in the Caribbean; its primary export crop is coffee. The Haitian currency is called "gourdes" from the name of the gourd vegetable. *Hayti* is the Indian name for the country; it translates to "land of the mountains." Haiti's mountain peaks exceed 8,000 feet in height! The only public university in Haiti is the University of Haiti in Port-au-Prince, founded in 1944.

Unsurprisingly, given the region, the national dish is rice served with beans. The cuisine is a fusion between Creole and French cooking styles. The story behind Soup Joumou is so interesting and important to the Haitian culture, I picked this great dish to make. Haiti was under French rule from 1625 until January 1st, 1804. Under French rule, Haitian slaves and the lower classes were forbidden to drink this soup. On January 1st, 1804 and every January 1st since, all Haitians, no matter where they are in the world, eat this dish in remembrance of their independence.

SOUP JOUMOU

INGREDIENTS:

1 Tbsp. Olive oil

1 cup onion (small dice)

6 cup water

1 cup butternut squash (peeled and cut into 1" cubes)

1 sweet potato (peeled 1" cubes)

2 carrots (2" cut)

1 celery (1" cut)

1½ cup cabbage (1" slice)

1–14 oz. can diced tomatoes (undrained)

1–14 oz. can red beans (rinsed and drained)

¼ tsp. crushed red pepper

½ tsp. cinnamon

¼ tsp. cloves

¼ tsp. nutmeg

Salt and pepper to taste

4 oz. spaghetti (broken into 2" pieces)

2 Tbsp. Parsley (sliced)

3 Tbsp. scallions (sliced thin)

DIRECTIONS:

Prepare all of the ingredients as directed. In a medium stock pot, heat the oil, add the onion, and sauté for 1 minute. Add the water and the squash to the pan, bring to a boil, and then reduce to medium heat for 10 minutes. Purée the squash mixture in a food processor and then return to the pan. Add all remaining ingredients except the spaghetti, parsley, and scallions. Bring the pot to a medium boil and then reduce the heat to low. During this process, you may need to add water. Cook for 10–15 minutes until the potatoes are crisp and tender. Add the spaghetti and cook for another 5–7 minutes until the pasta is al dente in texture. Serve in warm bowls and garnish with parsley and scallions.

REMMI NOTES: This pot of golden goodness is nothing but great comfort food. Need I say more? Add some crusty bread and you have a heavenly combination.

Just southwest of Haiti and across the Jamaica Channel is the third largest island in the Caribbean, where the average temperature is 80 degrees Fahrenheit. Jamaica is known for its snowy white sand beaches with more than 700 caves to explore. The island has a variety of culinary influences—African, French, Spanish, Chinese, British, and Indian food have all contributed to Jamaican cuisine. Reggae dance and music comes from Jamaica, as did the late Bob Marley, who was internationally known for his reggae music.

There is a style of cooking meats in Jamaica called "jerk." It can be either dry or wet, but either way has very spicy seasoning, which usually includes allspice and Scotch bonnet peppers. Ackee and Saltfish is one of the main dishes served in Jamaica. Ackee is a tree fruit which has been described as having a texture like butter. If this fruit is not handled properly in the ripening and cooking processes, it has toxins that can literally kill you. Ackee is banned by the U.S. FDA...so there's no Ackee and Saltfish on this menu. I do have a popular Jamaican seafood dish, Curry Shrimp and Rice, for you.

CURRY SHRIMP AND RICE

INGREDIENTS:

2 cups basmati rice (or else long grain—
  prepare as directed)

1½ lb. large shrimp (peeled and deveined
  with tails intact)

1½ Tbsp olive oil

1 medium size onion (medium dice)

2 garlic cloves (crushed)

¼ tsp. red pepper flakes

½ cup celery (medium dice)

2 tsp. curry powder

1½ cup tomatoes (medium dice)

1 green bell pepper (julienned)

1 cup coconut milk

1½ cup vegetable broth

Salt and pepper to taste

2 Tbsp. basil (chiffonade)

4 Tbsp. green onion (sliced thin on bias)

DIRECTIONS:

Prepare all of the ingredients as directed. In a medium pan, prepare the rice as directed. In a medium saucepan, heat the olive oil, and add the onion, garlic, red pepper flakes, celery, and curry. Sauté for 2 minutes. Add tomatoes, bell pepper, milk, and broth. Bring heat to a medium boil and then turn down and simmer for 8-10 minutes. Add the shrimp and cook 4-5 minutes more until the shrimp is cooked through. Serve with steamed rice and garnish with basil and green onion.

REMMI NOTES: This a is a very quick dish to make. Often it's served with a national rice dish that is called "rice and peas," which is rice is mixed with "pigeon peas" or kidney beans. Pigeon peas are difficult to find, but you can add a can of kidney beans to make this dish more authentic. This dish would go great with a cool and refreshing side of tropical sliced fruit like mango or papaya. Enjoy!

Leaving Jamaica, we sail east to our final island in the Greater Antilles. Puerto Rico is a popular vacation spot with more than 270 miles of beaches. The temperature is in the 70–80 degrees Fahrenheit range all year long. Its culture has been influenced by several others, including Spanish and African. Their cuisine uses many spices, making for very flavorful dishes. They highlight fresh foods in all of their meals. In Puerto Rico, the cuisine is known as *cocina criolla*, or "creole cuisine." Locals are very friendly and hospitable.

On special holidays and at most family celebrations, *Lechon Asado*, a whole roasted pig, will be the main fare. A famous place to have roasted pig is Guavate, located in the central mountains. The road leading to this area is *La Ruta De Lechon*, which translates to "Pork Highway." Along this highway, you can experience *Lechoneras*, which are rustic eateries featuring roasted pig. Local families often go to this area on weekends.

While I didn't bring you a *Lechon Asado* Family Feast, I have still brought you a delicious feast filled with many Puerto Rican favorites. Most meals start with a soup, and the most well-known soup is black bean. Besides roast pork, the locals love chicken, and *Arroz con Pollo* is the favored chicken and rice dish. Coconut is used often with dishes involving fruit.

PUERTO RICAN FAMILY FEAST

BLACK BEAN SOUP

Prep time: 15 minutes • Cook time: 15 minutes

INGREDIENTS:

1 Tbsp. olive oil

1 cup onion (medium dice, divided)

¼ cup celery (medium dice)

½ cup red bell pepper (medium dice)

1 tsp. garlic (minced)

2-14.5 oz cans black beans (undrained)

½ tsp. cumin

2 cups chicken broth (nonfat/low sodium/divided)

2 Tbsp. fresh parsley

1 Tbsp. jalapeño pepper (seeded and minced)

Salt and pepper to taste

½ cup yogurt (plain nonfat)

1 avocado (large dice)

½ cup cilantro leaves

DIRECTIONS:

In a medium saucepan, heat the oil and then sauté ¾ cup of the onion plus celery, bell pepper, and garlic for 1-2 minutes. Add beans, cumin, 1 cup chicken broth, parsley, jalapeño, and salt and pepper to taste. Bring to a boil, then turn down the heat to simmer for 15 minutes. Add more of the remaining chicken broth until the soup reaches your desired consistency. Serve soup with the remaining onion, yogurt, avocado, and cilantro as sides for garnish.

REMMI NOTES: Using canned beans, this soup is so easy to make!

COLE SLAW WITH LIME VINAIGRETTE

INGREDIENTS:

8 cups green cabbage (thinly sliced)

1 apple (medium dice)

¼ cup green onion (sliced on diagonal)

1 jalapeño pepper (small/seeds removed/ minced)

3 Tbsp. cilantro (sliced)

2 Tbsp. parsley (sliced)

3 Tbsp. light oil (safflower or canola)

3 Tbsp. lime juice

2 tsp. honey

Salt and pepper to taste

DIRECTIONS:

Prepare ingredients as directed. In a medium bowl, mix the cabbage, apple, green onion, jalapeño pepper, cilantro, and parsley. In separate bowl, mix the oil, lime juice, honey, and salt and pepper. Toss the coleslaw with the dressing.

TOMATO SALSA AND AVOCADO CREAM

SALSA INGREDIENTS:

Salsa:

2 cup fresh tomatoes (medium dice)

¼ cup onion (medium dice)

1 tsp. garlic (minced)

½ cup cilantro leaves

1 jalapeño (seeded and diced small)

1 Tbsp. lime juice

1 tsp. olive oil

Salt and pepper to taste

Avocado Cream:

1 ripe avocado (pitted and skin removed)

½ cup sour cream (nonfat)

1 Tbsp. lime juice

Salt and pepper to taste

DIRECTIONS:

Salsa: Prepare all of the ingredients as directed. In small bowl, combine all ingredients.

Avocado Cream: In small bowl, lightly mash the avocado. In a separate bowl, combine the sour cream, lime juice, salt and pepper. Fold mashed avocado into the cream mixture.

ARROZ CON POLLO

INGREDIENTS:

1 whole fryer chicken (cut into pieces, breast cut in half)

1 tsp. paprika

Salt and pepper

1½ Tbsp. olive oil (divided)

1 onion (large to small dice as preferred)

2 cups red and green bell peppers (medium dice; 1 cup each color)

1 jalapeño pepper (medium to small dice as preferred)

2 garlic cloves (minced)

2 cups basmati rice or jasmine rice

3¼ cup low sodium chicken broth

1 tomato (large to medium dice as preferred)

½ tsp. turmeric

Salt and pepper to taste

¾ cup frozen peas

¼ cup flat leaf parsley (sliced)

1 lime (sliced in wedges)

DIRECTIONS:

Prepare ingredients as directed. Season the chicken pieces with the salt, pepper, and paprika. In a large pan heat 1 Tbsp. of olive oil, then add the chicken and sauté until golden brown on both sides. When the chicken is done, remove it from the pan and set it aside. Drain any grease from the pan. Add the remaining olive oil with the onions, peppers, and garlic. Sauté for 1–2 minutes. Add the rice to the mixture and sauté for 1–2 minutes more. Add the chicken broth, tomato, turmeric, salt and pepper. Bring to a boil, then cover the pan and turn heat to low. Simmer for 15 minutes. Take the lid off of the pan and add the peas on top of the rice, then add the chicken. Place the lid back on the pan for 10–15 minutes until the rice and chicken are fully cooked. After the dish is fully cooked, remove the chicken from the pan. Fluff the rice and add the parsley. Place a mound of rice on individual plates and serve with one or two pieces of chicken with the salsa, avocado cream, and lime wedges.

COCONUT MANGO FRUIT COCKTAIL

INGREDIENTS:

3 cups mango (large dice)

2 cups pineapple (large dice)

¼ cup dried cherries

¼ cup fresh coconut

Nutmeg

DIRECTIONS:

Prepare ingredients as directed. In a medium bowl, mix the mango, pineapple, and dried cherries. Serve in individual bowls and sprinkle each with the coconut and just a tiny dash of nutmeg.

REMMI NOTES: I love this feast because I enjoy Arroz con Pollo. I published this recipe in my first cookbook but just had to offer it again. Serving this feast with the salsa and avocado cream makes this dish exceptional. I know I am serving up a lot of fruit recipes for dessert, but why not—it's simple, delicious, and hopefully is getting you to try new combinations of fruits. Plus, fruit is healthy! Enjoy the feast!

The many small islands collectively known as the Lesser Antilles are found south of Cuba. We will taste the cuisine of two of these intriguing islands, starting with Barbados. Barbados' name comes from "Los Barbados" in Portuguese, which translates to "Bearded Fig Tree." Established in 1639, the Parliament of Barbados is the third oldest in the entire world. The grapefruit is a hybrid fruit which was invented by Barbadians. "Flying fish" are a common oceanic sight off the coast of Barbados. It is considered the most advanced Caribbean island country.

The national dish of Barbados is Cou Cou, which is like a creamy polenta with okra and flying fish and prepared with several different cooking techniques and usually one or two spicy sauces. Another Barbadian staple is a cucumber dish that makes for a simple but sweet and spicy side. Spice is prevalent in the cuisine, and this great side dish helps to cool the flavors of the rest of the meal down. For special occasions, "pudding" and "souse" are served with "a pickle," and what I am offering here is a recipe for "A Pickle." But if you want to make "souse," a boiled pig head, accompanied by "pudding," a mashed potato dish enclosed in pig's belly, you are on your own! Instead, let's try some delicious street food: Chicken and Potato Roti!

BARBADIAN PICKLED CUCUMBER SALAD ("A PICKLE")

INGREDIENTS:

2 cucumbers (unpeeled and sliced
   very thin)
½ cup onion (sliced thin)
1 Tbsp. canola oil

2½ Tbsp. lime juice
⅛ tsp. nutmeg
Salt and pepper to taste
2 Tbsp. parsley (sliced)

DIRECTIONS:

Prepare all of the ingredients as specified above. In medium bowl, mix all ingredients.
Serve chilled.

REMMI NOTES: Sometimes simple turns into great. This recipe for "A Pickle" caught my attention because I love to make simple salads out of cucumbers. I don't know why I love cucumbers so much, but they are my favorite, right behind strawberries, which are my all-time favorite food. Come to think of it, I combine strawberries and cucumbers in a lot of my dishes!

CHICKEN AND POTATO ROTI

ROTI

INGREDIENTS:

2 cups flour

¼ tsp. baking soda

½ tsp. salt

¾ cup water

¼ cup oil

DIRECTIONS:

Mix the dry ingredients and knead with water in a bowl. Once the dough is mixed, place on a floured surface and knead the dough for 10 minutes. Place a moist towel on the dough and let it rest for 30 minutes.

Divide the dough into 4 sections and roll into ball shapes. Prepare a floured surface. With a rolling pin, roll out each ball in the shape of a circle. They should be approximately 7–8"s wide. Brush both sides of the roti with oil and place in a heated skillet on medium-high heat. Lightly crisp each side of the roti. Serve warm.

Note: You can make the roti ahead of time and just reheat for a few seconds in the microwave.

CHICKEN AND POTATO

INGREDIENTS:

2 Tbsp. oil

1 onion (medium, sliced thin)

2 garlic cloves (crushed)

½ cup green pepper (sliced thin)

1 lb. chicken (light or dark meat or combination, 1" dice)

2 potatoes (Yukon gold preferred, medium dice)

2-3 Tbsp. curry powder

2 tsp. cumin

1 tsp. turmeric

¼ tsp. nutmeg

¼ tsp. crushed red pepper

2-3 cups chicken broth

Salt and pepper to taste

¼ cup parsley (chopped)

1 cup tomatoes (large dice)

DIRECTIONS:

Prepare all of the ingredients as directed. Oil a medium sauce pan and sauté the onion, garlic, and green pepper for 1-2 minutes. Add the chicken to the pan and stir fry for 4-5 minutes. Add the potatoes, then add the spices: curry, cumin, turmeric, nutmeg, and crushed red pepper. Stir the spices in, then add enough chicken broth to cover the meat and potato mixture. Add desired amount of salt and pepper. Bring the dish to boil and then reduce heat to simmer. Cook for 20-30 minutes or until the potatoes are tender. Prepare a roti recipe. You can serve this dish in bowls with roti as a side, or it is also delicious with the mixture rolled into the roti.

Note: You may substitute 4 flour tortillas or pita bread for the roti if short on time. Make sure to toast them in a pan before adding the filling.

REMMI NOTES: The Chicken and Potato Roti dish is like magical comfort food...I so love this dish! There are hundreds of recipes you can draw from to make roti. It is worth it, especially since it does not take a lot of time to make. Add *your* favorite veggies to make this dish your own—it's perfect for that.

Trinidad and Tobago is a two-island country in the southern part of the Lesser Antilles island chain. Their most well-known celebration is the Trinidad and Tobago Carnival, which is celebrated the Monday and Tuesday before Ash Wednesday. An important part of the festival is dressing up in costumes. Islanders use mud, paint, and oil to create bright costumes. Another notable part of the festival is the parade. The parade embodies the most vibrant parts of the culture of Trinidad and Tobago: music, dance, and food. There are also calypso music and dance competitions.

The cuisine of Trinidad and Tobago blends Creole, Indian, African, French, and Spanish influences. These diverse origins have given rise to dishes with robust and unique flavors, many of which contain fresh fruits that are readily accessible, like papayas. The combination of bold spices and sweet citrus makes these dishes simple to make, yet still imbued with delicious flavor.

CARIBBEAN FLANK STEAK

INGREDIENTS:

1½ lb. flank steak

¼ tsp. cloves

¼ tsp. cinnamon

¼ tsp. nutmeg

½ tsp. crushed red pepper

½ tsp. thyme

½ tsp. sugar

Pepper to taste

DIRECTIONS:

In a small bowl, mix cloves, cinnamon, nutmeg, red pepper, thyme, sugar, and pepper. Place the meat on a plate and rub it with the dry spices on both sides. Grill the steak to desired doneness, then thinly slice it against the grain. Serve with papaya salsa (see recipe below).

REMMI NOTES: You have to make sure that you rub the spices on the meat well, because that is what gives this steak its flavor! The salsa helps to add a fresher bite to this dish and works great with the spices on the steak.

PAPAYA SALSA

INGREDIENTS:

1 papaya (seeded and peeled, 2" dice)

½ cucumber (medium dice)

1 red bell pepper (medium dice)

1 small sweet onion (medium dice)

½ jalapeño pepper (seeded and minced)

1 Tbsp. garlic (minced)

3 Tbsp. cilantro (sliced

¼ cup pineapple juice

¼ cup lime juice

Salt and pepper to taste

DIRECTIONS:

Prepare ingredients as specified in ingredient list, mix all ingredients, and refrigerate until ready to serve.

REMMI NOTES: I love to create salsas; they are easy to make and you can be very creative. The seeds of the papaya are edible—in some cuisines they use them in place of peppercorns. Salsas are also great to serve with different meats, so experiment!

"You don't have to cook fancy or complicated masterpieces—just good food from fresh ingredients."

—Julia Child

CONTINENT

OF SOUTH

AMERICA

"People should open themselves to other cuisines. There are a lot of hidden secrets all over the world."
—**Yotam Ottolenghi**

From Trinidad and Tobago, we travel south across the Caribbean Sea to our next continent, where we will explore the cuisine of five countries. The South American continent, which is rich in petroleum, copper, gold, and silver, is located in the western hemisphere. The Andes, the longest mountain range in the world, is found in South America, as is the world's largest waterfall, Venezuela's Angel Falls. Brazil is the largest country on the continent, and the Amazon rainforest, the world's largest, is located there. We will travel to five South American countries starting with the northernmost country on the continent.

Colombia borders the Pacific Ocean and the Caribbean Sea and is connected to Central America by the Isthmus of Panama. Bogotá is its capital. Colombia was named after the last name of the explorer Christopher Columbus. They are the largest producer of emeralds and they are internationally known for their coffee. Cali is the salsa dancing center of the world. The internationally famous singer Shakira is from Colombia.

Colombian dining etiquette is very formal. It is impolite to start eating until the host says "Buen Provecho!" Hands are to be visible at all times while eating. Utensils are used with the fork held in the left hand and the knife in the right hand. It is expected to try all foods that are offered, and it is also considered polite to leave a small amount of food on your plate. Meat dominates the cuisine along with fresh fruits. A common side dish is arepa, which is a cornmeal bread that is served with most meals. "Bandeja Bogotáno" is a common Colombian platter ensemble consisting of beef, pork belly, chorizo, beans, rice, plantains, fried eggs, and avocado...now that's a spread!

SUDADO DE POLLO (COLOMBIAN CHICKEN STEW)

Prep time: 20 minutes • Cook time: 1 hour

INGREDIENTS:

2 Tbsp. olive oil

6 chicken thighs (boneless and skinless)

1 medium onion (large dice)

½ cup carrots (1" slices)

½ tsp. garlic (minced)

1 large tomato (large dice)

½ tsp. garlic powder

1 tsp. cumin

Pinch of saffron

1½ Tbsp. cilantro (finely chopped)

½ cup Yukon Gold potatoes (skins left on; quartered)

2 cups chicken broth

DIRECTIONS:

Prepare all of the ingredients as specified in the ingredients list. To a large pan at high heat, add oil, then brown the chicken on both sides. Once the chicken has been browned, add onion, carrots, and garlic. Sauté for about 3 minutes. Add the tomato, garlic powder, cumin, saffron, cilantro, and potatoes. Pour in the chicken broth, adding more if necessary to cover all vegetables and chicken. Bring to a boil, then lower heat to simmer for about 40-45 minutes or until vegetables are tender and chicken is cooked through. Serve and enjoy!

REMMI NOTES: This classic Colombian dish has such bold flavors! It is very important to develop the sauce really well, because that's where all the flavors really are. If you don't have saffron, you can substitute about a ¼ tsp. of turmeric, which doesn't give you the flavor of the saffron, but does give you the color! This warm dish is one of my favorites on cold, rainy days because it warms your stomach. It is best served over white rice, so the rice can soak up the broth and all of the delicious flavor!

Due south from Colombia is Peru, which is bordered by Ecuador, Colombia, Brazil, Bolivia, and Chile. The Peruvian portion of the famous Amazon Rainforest fills about 69 percent of the country. Peru has the second largest portion of the Amazon Rainforest, while Brazil contains the largest chunk. Peru's landscapes are as well-known as its history. Machu Picchu is the site of the ancient ruins of Peru's Quechua ancestors and is the country's most popular tourist spot. This Incan citadel is found deep in the mountainous Andes; the journey there is not easy, but the historical site, along with breathtaking views, make the trek worth it.

Peruvian cuisine has become increasingly more well-known in recent years. Its influences range from the country's indigenous Incan roots to the cuisines of Spain, China, and Italy, and Peru is becoming a South American food hub. One of the staples of Peruvian cuisine is quinoa. Many of their dishes have big flavors due to their range of chilis and other spices used.

PERUVIAN BEEF AND RICE TIMBALE

INGREDIENTS:

2 cups jasmine rice or basmati rice (uncooked)

4 cups water

1 cup frozen peas

2 Tbsp. olive oil (divided)

1 large sweet potato (peeled, medium dice; roasted)

2 garlic cloves (minced)

½ cup onion (small dice)

1 lb. ground beef

4 oz. can Hatch chilis

1 14 oz. can diced tomatoes

1 tsp. paprika

1 tsp. cumin

¼ cup fresh parsley (sliced and divided)

Salt and pepper to taste

4 hard-boiled eggs (sliced)

Cooking spray

DIRECTIONS:

Prepare the rice according to the package instructions. Add the frozen peas to the rice 5 minutes before the rice is finished cooking. Prepare the sweet potato as directed and place on a baking sheet. Drizzle 1 Tbsp. of the olive oil onto the diced potato, then bake potato in 400 degree oven for 15 minutes or until tender. In medium pan, sauté the onion and garlic in the remaining Tbsp. of olive oil for 2 minutes. Add the ground beef and sauté until beef is no longer pink. Drain any grease from the beef. Add chilis, tomatoes, paprika, cumin, 2 Tbsp. of the parsley, and sweet potato. Simmer for 10 minutes. Spray a 6-8 oz. bowl with cooking spray. Fill ⅓ of the bowl with rice, followed by a layer of eggs, one of meat, and then another layer of rice. Press the mixture firmly into the mold. Turn the bowl upside down on serving plate. Prepare additional servings on separate plates. Garnish with the remaining parsley.

REMMI NOTES: This dish is so much fun to prepare, especially when you plate it! It's very important to make sure you pack your bowl tightly so that the dish keeps its shape when you turn it over. I have only ever used a bowl, but I'm sure you could use other shapes if you wanted! The flavors in the dish are outstanding, and the white rice helps to hold some of the flavor and soak up the sauce.

"Cooking well doesn't mean cooking fancy."

—Julia Child

Our next stop south is Bolivia, which is a landlocked country bordered by Peru, Chile, Brazil, Paraguay, and Argentina. Lake Titicaca is the highest navigable lake in the world in terms of elevation. The Bolivian region of Santa Cruz has the largest butterfly sanctuary in the world. The world's largest salt flat is located in Salar de Uyuni, Bolivia. Bolivia is also the home of large cities such as Santa Cruz de la Sierra, El Alto, and La Paz.

For Bolivians, lunch is their biggest meal of the day. Dinner, in comparison, is usually light and is served late in the evening. It is considered bad luck to receive food or drink from hand to hand; these are served from the table or a tray. Potatoes, beans, and corn are the mainstays of their diet. In fact, a national dish called "Plato Paceño" is a plate of potatoes, beans, and corn, sometimes served with cheese. There are over 4,000 varieties of potatoes in Bolivia.

PAPAS RELLENAS (STUFFED POTATOES)

Prep time: 30 minutes • Cook time: 25 minutes

INGREDIENTS:

4 large potatoes (peeled, large dice)

3 Tbsp. flour

1 egg

2 Tbsp. olive oil

1 lb. ground beef

¾ cup onion (small dice)

¾ cup red pepper (small dice)

1 garlic (minced)

8 oz. tomato sauce

1 tsp. cumin

¼ tsp. red pepper flakes

½ cup olives (green or black)

1 Tbsp. parsley

3 eggs (hard-boiled, large dice)

Salt and Pepper to taste

2 eggs (lightly beaten)

1 cup bread crumbs (plain)

Salsa

DIRECTIONS:

Preheat oven to 425 degrees. Prepare all of the ingredients as directed. Boil the potatoes for 15–20 minutes, then drain and mash. Once slightly cooled, mix the mashed potatoes with flour and egg. Set aside. In a medium saucepan, heat oil, then add the meat, onion, red pepper, and garlic. Cook on medium low until meat is cooked through. Add the tomato sauce, cumin, red pepper flakes, and olives and heat for 5 minutes. Remove from heat and fold in the hard-boiled eggs and salt and pepper to taste. Place a piece of parchment paper on a large baking sheet. Allow meat mixture and mashed potatoes to cool before assembling. Place beaten eggs and breadcrumbs in 2 small bowls. Using an ice cream scoop, place a serving of the potatoes in the palm of your hand. Flatten the potato mixture, make a dent, and place 1½ Tbsp. of meat mixture. With wet hands, fold the potato around the meat mixture, forming a ball. Chill or freeze balls for 10-15 minutes. Dip the potato ball in the egg mixture, roll in crumb mixture, and place on lined baking sheet. Repeat. Place in preheated oven for 25 minutes or until golden.

REMMI NOTES: This dish is normally prepared by deep frying the potato balls, but I elected to try a healthier version by using a baking technique instead. Papas Rellenas is one of those recipes where you can bring together many different combinations of ingredients. They are delicious with meats, but they can be just as delicious either using just vegetables or bringing together the right combination of vegetables and dried fruits for a sweet and savory taste. To complete the presentation of these delectable delights, serve with salsa, ketchup, or a simple fresh salad.

Moving south from Bolivia, Chile is one of the most stable and prosperous countries in South America. Santiago is its capital. Chile is known for its fine wines and is the ninth largest wine-producing nation in the world by volume. It is also the largest producer and exporter of copper in the world. Penguins not only live in Antarctica, they also live in southern Chile. Chile's territory contains Easter Island, the most isolated inhabited island in the world. Its Atacama Desert is the driest place on earth.

Due to Chile's long coastline, seafood is plentiful and is a central ingredient in Chilean cuisine. Maize, quinoa, olives, and potatoes are staple foods. Popular street foods include empanadas and humitas, which are made of a corn and onion paste steamed in corn husks. Chileans like sweet flavors, and they tend not to care for really spicy foods.

CHILEAN PASTEL DE CHOCLO (CORN PIE)

Prep time: 35 minutes • Cook time: 40 minutes

INGREDIENTS:

Meat Mixture:
2 Tbsp. oil
1 lb. ground beef
½ cup onions (small dice)
½ cup beef broth
1 tsp. cumin
2 tsp. chile powder
¼ cup parsley
1 Tbsp. flour
Salt and pepper to taste
3 eggs (hard-boiled and sliced)
1 cup black olives

Corn Topping:
¼ cup butter (melted)
4 cup frozen corn
½ cup half and half (for lower fat, substitute ½ cup dairy or soy yogurt)
2 Tbsp. sugar
Salt and pepper to taste
4 eggs (separated, with whites beaten until stiff peaks form)
¼ cup basil (chiffonade)
Cooking spray

DIRECTIONS:

Preheat oven to 375 degrees. Prepare all of the ingredients as directed. In a medium pan, heat the oil, and add the ground beef and onion. Cook until the meat is no longer pink. Add the cumin, chili powder, parsley, flour, and salt and pepper to taste. Bring the mixture to a boil, reduce heat to simmer, and cook for 5-10 minutes until the sauce thickens. Spray a medium casserole dish with cooking spray and layer the meat mixture with the hard-boiled eggs and olives. In a blender, add the butter, corn, half and half, sugar, and salt and pepper to taste. Blend the ingredients together quickly, keeping the corn texture chunky. Pour the corn mixture in a bowl, add the egg yolks, and blend. Fold the beaten egg whites into the corn mixture. Spread the corn mixture onto the meat mixture, then place it in the oven for 35–40 minutes until the corn topping is golden. Garnish with fresh basil.

REMMI NOTES: This corn pie has become one of my family's favorites. I guess this is not a surprise, since my cottage pie is one of their favorites as well. This great pie has really simple ingredients...basic cookery that just makes you feel good! Love it!

Argentina, our last country in the continent of South America, is due east of Chile. It is the third largest producer of meat in the world. The Argentine "pampas" are flat grassy plains used to herd sheep and cattle which cover the north and central areas of Argentina. Buenos Aires is the capital. The renowned Argentine tango is a dance that originated in Buenos Aires and Montevideo in the late 1880s. Argentina is known for having an internationally top-rated soccer team. There is also a national sport called "Pato," meaning "duck," which is played on horseback and contains elements of basketball.

"Asada," barbecued or grilled steak, is the national dish. Argentines love steak, and their meat is considered top-quality. Their cuisine has Spanish and Italian influences. *Dulce de leche* sauce is added to most desserts to sweeten them; "dulce de leche," literally "sweet of milk," means "caramel." Empanadas are another favorite and staple in their cuisine.

FLANK STEAK WITH CHIMICHURRI SAUCE

Prep time: 20 minutes • Cook time: 15 minutes

INGREDIENTS:

2 Tbsp. olive oil

2 lbs. flank steak

1 large onion (½" slices)

¼ cup onion (chopped)

1½ cups parsley (chopped)

2 tsp. garlic (minced)

3 Tbsp. lemon juice

3 Tbsp. red wine vinegar

½ tsp. red pepper flakes.

Salt and pepper to taste

3 cups arugula (or baby lettuces)

DIRECTIONS:

Prepare ingredients as directed. Brush the steak with olive oil and heavily salt and pepper it. Place on a hot grill and cook to desired doneness. Remove from heat and set aside. To make the chimichurri sauce, in a medium bowl add the remaining ingredients except for the arugula. Slice meat against the grain in thin strips. To serve, place a serving of steak on a bed of arugula and spoon desired amount of sauce over it.

REMMI NOTES: What I love about this dish is the freshness the sauce brings to the dish. Add a loaf of crusty bread, and you have a simple but elegant meal!

CONTINENT OF EUROPE

"Food brings people together on many different levels. It's nourishment of the soul and body; it's truly love."
—**Giada De Laurentiis**

Returning to the northern hemisphere, we travel on to Europe, a continent filled with diverse cultures. Despite being the second smallest continent, it is the third *largest* continent in terms of population! Europe is also home to both the largest and smallest countries in the world—there are over fifty countries and sovereign states located in Europe!

Iceland, an island in the North Atlantic Ocean, is considered to be part of Europe, though it is not a member of the European Union. To put it in perspective, flying from London to Iceland would take three hours. Reykjavik is the northernmost capital city in the world. Family names are generally not much used in Iceland, and the telephone book has everyone listed by their first name. The population of Iceland is a bit over 300,000. The majority of the country's electricity and heating is accomplished through hydroelectric and geothermal power.

Iceland has some interesting delicacies: raw puffin heart, sheep head, fermented shark, pickled whale blubber, and sheep hearts cooked in wine are a few of the favorites. Iceland is known for its tender lamb and abundance of fish, as well as for the sweet dairy product called skyr.

COD EN PAPILLOTE WITH LEMON EGG SAUCE

Prep time: 25 minutes • Cook time: 20 minutes

INGREDIENTS:

Parchment paper (four 12" x 14" pieces
   of parchment paper, heart shaped)
4-6-8 oz. cod fillets (washed and
   patted dry)
2 Tbsp. olive oil
1 lemon (sliced)
1 cup frozen peas

4 sprigs parsley
Salt and pepper
5 Tbsp. butter
3 Tbsp. lemon juice
3 eggs (hard-boiled, large chop)
Parsley

DIRECTIONS:

Cut 4 pieces of parchment paper to specified size and shape. On each, place a cod fillet at the fold and in the center. Place 2 lemon slices on each fillet, then evenly divide the peas across each fillet and add salt and pepper to taste. Divide the parsley sprigs and top each fillet, then drizzle with olive oil. Starting with the open side (the top of the heart), make 1" folds to seal the packet and twist the end of the heart to seal. Place packets on a baking sheet and place in oven at 400 degrees for 20 minutes. While the cod is in the oven, melt the butter, lemon juice, and chopped eggs in a small pan and warm. Remove the cod en papillote, and use shears to cut an "X" in the top of each packet. Evenly divide the lemon egg sauce between the packets, garnish with more parsley, and serve.

REMMI NOTES: En papillote is my favorite technique for cooking fish. It is very easy to prepare, and there is basically no mess, since the entire dish is in the parchment pocket. It makes for a beautiful presentation of the food. Make sure to fold the paper tightly when you are wrapping the fish to ensure that no steam escapes! I was thrilled to run across this sauce, which incorporates EGGS! International cuisines contain myriad with ideas on how to use eggs differently. This is a fun dish for anyone to make.

ICELANDIC POTATOES

Prep time: 10 minutes • Cook time: 40 minutes

INGREDIENTS:

1½ lb. Yukon Gold potatoes (unpeeled)

2 Tbsp. olive oil

1 cup baby onions (peeled)

3 Tbsp. brown sugar

3 Tbsp. butter

1½ Tbsp. water

Salt and pepper to taste

2 Tbsp. fresh sage leaves (sliced)

DIRECTIONS:

Cook the potatoes in water for 12-15 minutes or until tender and drain. In a medium saucepan and on medium heat, add the olive oil. Once the oil is warmed, add the baby onions, turn heat to low, and sauté for 5 minutes. Add the water, butter, and sugar, and heat, stirring occasionally, until mixture is melted and combined. Add the potatoes and salt and pepper to taste, then sauté in the caramel sauce for 10 minutes. Garnish with sage.

REMMI NOTES: This potato dish is incredibly delicious. I tend to shy away from a lot of butter and sugar, but the sauce for these potatoes is, luscious. The sweetness of the potatoes is tempered a bit by the onions and sage, making the dish both sweet and savory. Enjoy!

Moving inland, our next stop is Norway. Norway is located in northern Europe bordering Sweden, Finland, and Russia. Its long coast borders on multiple bodies of water, including the North Sea, the North Atlantic, the Barents Sea, and the Skagerrak Inlet. The country is the world's largest exporter of salmon, and Norwegians are responsible for introducing salmon to the Japanese as an ingredient for sushi. Norway's national symbol is the lion. When an author publishes a book in Norway, the government purchases 1,000 copies of each title and then distributes the books to their libraries. Norway is the wealthiest country in the world. Norwegian public universities are free to attend, regardless of nationality or citizenship.

NORWEGIAN FAMILY FEAST

GREEN SALAD WITH LEMON VINAIGRETTE

Prep time: 15 minutes

INGREDIENTS:

1 large head of Boston lettuce (torn in large pieces)
2 Tbsp. cider vinegar
1 Tbsp. lemon juice
1 tsp. sugar

1½ tsp. half and half (for lower fat, substitute dairy or soy yogurt)
2 Tbsp. fresh dill
Salt and pepper to taste

DIRECTIONS:

Prepare all of the ingredients as directed. Place the lettuce leaves in a medium bowl. In a small bowl, mix vinegar, lemon juice, sugar, and half and half. When ready to serve, toss the salad with the dressing. Add salt and pepper to taste and garnish with fresh dill.

POTATO DUMPLINGS (KLUB) WITH PEAS

Prep time: 15 minutes • Cook time: 30 minutes

INGREDIENTS:

4 medium potatoes (for 4 cups total when peeled and grated)

1 egg

1½ cup flour (may need additional flour for right consistency)

Salt to taste

2 cups chicken broth

2 cups water

1 cup frozen peas

2 Tbsp. parsley (sliced)

1 green onion (sliced)

3 Tbsp. butter

Pepper

DIRECTIONS:

Prepare ingredients as specified in the ingredients list. Place the potatoes in large bowl and mix in the egg. Salt as desired. Gradually mix in the flour until the mixture holds together. Bring broth and water to boil using a large pot. Form the dumpling mixture into 2½" balls. Gently place the dumplings in the boiling water. Then turn down the heat to simmer and cook for 30 minutes. Test one dumpling to make sure it is cooked through. Add the frozen peas to the pot and cook for 2 more minutes. Remove the dumplings and peas with slotted spoon, and place on a platter. Garnish with the parsley and onion. Drizzle the melted butter onto the dish. Finish with fresh pepper. Serve warm.

SWEET AND SOUR CABBAGE

INGREDIENTS:

2 Tbsp. olive oil

½ cup onion (sliced thin)

2 apples (½" slices)

½ cup apple cider vinegar

¼ cup honey

¼ cup water

8 cup red cabbage (sliced thin)

Salt and pepper to taste

2 Tbsp. butter

¼ tsp. caraway seed (optional)

DIRECTIONS:

Prepare ingredients as directed. In a medium stock pot add the oil and heat to medium. Add the onions and apples and sauté for 2 minutes. Add all remaining ingredients except the butter and caraway. Cover the pot for 10–15 minutes and heat until the cabbage is crisp but tender. Remove from heat and add the butter and caraway seeds. Note: In other recipes, this dish is often cooked for a longer period of time, but I prefer the crisp-tender texture instead. Cook longer if you like your cabbage more tender.

BAKED LEMON COD

INGREDIENTS:

Cooking spray

1½ lb. cod cutlets (washed)

¼ cup flour

Salt and pepper to taste

1 lemon slice (per cutlet)

Butter (one thin slice per cutlet)

1 Tbsp. lemon juice

½ tsp. lemon zest

1 cup cherry tomatoes

4 Tbsp. almonds

1 green onion (sliced thin on the bias)

DIRECTIONS:

Prepare all of the ingredients as specified in the ingredients list. Preheat your oven to 350 degrees. Prepare a baking pan with cooking spray. Lightly coat the cutlets with flour and salt and pepper to taste. Place the cutlets on baking pan and top each with a slice of lemon and a slice of butter. Drizzle cutlets with lemon juice. Distribute zest on cutlets. Place in oven and bake for 10 minutes. Remove from oven; evenly distribute almonds on the cutlets and scatter the tomatoes. Return to the oven for an additional 10 minutes or until the cod is cooked but flaky. Remove from oven and garnish with green onions. Serve immediately.

PARSLEY POTATOES

INGREDIENTS:

1½ lbs. baby new potatoes (washed)

2–3 Tbsp. butter

2 Tbsp. parsley (sliced)

DIRECTIONS:

Prepare all of the ingredients as directed. Place the potatoes in a medium pan and cover with cold water. Heat to boiling, then turn the heat down to medium and cook the potatoes for 15 minutes. Potatoes are ready when easily pierced with a fork. Drain potatoes and place in a medium serving bowl. Add the butter, parsley, and salt and pepper and toss to combine. Serve warm with the meatballs.

NORWEGIAN MEATBALLS AND GRAVY (KJØTTBOLLER)

INGREDIENTS:

Cooking spray
1 egg
¼ tsp. nutmeg
¼ tsp. allspice
½ tsp. dry mustard
1½ lb. ground beef
½ lb. ground pork
1 cup mashed potatoes
½ cup panko
½ cup milk
Salt and pepper to taste

⅓ cup flour
1 Tbsp. olive oil
½ cup onion (sliced)
1½ cup beef broth
3 Tbsp. water
1½ Tbsp. cornstarch
Salt and pepper to taste
½ cup half and half (for lower fat,
    substitute ½ cup dairy or soy yogurt)
2 Tbsp. parsley (sliced)

DIRECTIONS:

Preheat oven to 400 degrees. Prepare a baking sheet with cooking spray. In a medium bowl mix the egg, nutmeg, allspice, and dry mustard. Add the two meats and mix. Add the mashed potatoes, panko, and milk and combine with the meat mixture. Add desired amount of salt and pepper. Form meat into 1½" balls, roll in flour, and place on the baking sheet. When finished, place meatballs in oven and cook for 15–20 minutes. While the meatballs are cooking, prepare the gravy. In a small saucepan, add the oil and heat to medium. Add the onions and sauté for 2 minutes. Stir in the beef broth and bring to medium boil. Combine the cornstarch with the water and add it to the broth. Add salt and pepper and turn heat to low. Cook for 5 minutes until thickened. When ready to serve, add the half and half to the gravy. Place meatballs on a serving platter; top meatballs with gravy and garnish with parsley. Serve warm with the Lemon Parsley Potatoes.

BLUEBERRY STRAWBERRY TROLL CREAM

Prep time: 20 minutes

INGREDIENTS:

1 cup blueberries (reserve 2 Tbsp.
   for garnish)
½ cup strawberries (sliced in half;
   reserve 2 berries)

½ cup sugar
2 egg whites
4 mint leaves

DIRECTIONS:

Prepare all of the ingredients as directed. In a food processor or blender, combine the strawberries and blueberries until fully mixed. In a separate bowl, use a mixer to whip the egg whites on high speed until soft peaks are formed. Lower to a medium speed and gradually add the sugar until all sugar is combined. Continue whipping egg whites and sugar until stiff peaks form. Place the strawberry and blueberry mixture in a large bowl and fold in the egg whites. Divide equally into four individual serving dishes, and garnish with the remaining berries and mint leaves.

REMMI NOTES: Family celebration meals consist of several meat dishes and many sides and sweets. "Ribbe," a roast of pork belly is most common along with smoked lamb ribs, turkey, ham, and some dishes made with fish. Norwegians eat a lot of potatoes with their meals. Cod dishes are among the favorites. I may not have included all the right sides in my family feast, but these tried and true recipes have become my favorite dishes. So if you make all of these dishes, you will have made a feast's worth of scrumptious foods. Berries are frequently served in dessert dishes. There is one berry that is unique to the region, the "cloudberry," which is grown wild yet is so loved. The berry has a tart taste when ripe, but when it is overripe, it becomes creamy like a yogurt. For the Troll Cream recipe, I had to substitute lingonberries with blueberries. Okay, so I *am* talking a lot about berries—I would love to try both of these unique berries, and yes…I love my berries.

To reach Finland from Norway, we travel across Sweden and the Gulf of Bothnia. The national animal of Finland is the brown bear. Finns are the world's biggest coffee drinkers! Finland is also known as "the Land of the Midnight Sun" because during the summer, the sun shines day and night. There are over 180,000 Finnish lakes. Helsinki is the largest city as well as the capital.

In Finland, staple crops include potatoes and grains. Fish is also common in Finnish dishes; a few fish that Finns enjoy are salmon, whitefish, and herring. Meat is a large part of their diet as well. Most often, they eat smoked ham, though on occasion reindeer meat is on the menu. One of their most popular dishes is "Kaalikääryleet." Kaalikääryleet are cabbage rolls, usually stuffed with beef and rice and wrapped in cabbage. Potatoes are served with this dish, either boiled or mashed, and sometimes berry sauce as well as an optional garnish.

CABBAGE ROLLS (KAALIKÄÄRYLEET) WITH CRANBERRY SAUCE

Prep time: 25 minutes • Cook time: 1 hour 10 minutes

INGREDIENTS:

1 green cabbage (cored)

1 onion (sliced thin)

½ cup rice

1 cup water for rice

½ cup green onion (small dice)

½ cup half and half (for lower fat, substitute ½ cup dairy or soy yogurt)

¼ tsp. nutmeg

½ tsp. marjoram

1 lb. ground chuck

1 egg

½ cup water

¼ cup maple syrup

8 oz. cranberries

⅓ cup orange juice

⅓ cup dark corn syrup

Zest of orange

Dash cinnamon

¼ tsp. ground cardamon

Salt and pepper to taste

½ lb. bacon (cooked; in 1" pieces)

¼ cup parsley (sliced)

DIRECTIONS:

Preheat oven to 350 degrees. Cook the rice in 1 cup of water for 7 minutes, then drain; prepare all other ingredients as specified in ingredients list. Place the cored cabbage in pan and cover halfway with water. Bring to a boil and cook for 5 minutes. Remove from the water and pull 10–12 outer leaves for the cabbage rolls. Slice remaining cabbage in 1" lengths and place in casserole dish. Slice onion thin and scatter over the cabbage in the dish. In a medium bowl, mix the rice, green onions, half and half, nutmeg, and marjoram. Add ground chuck and mix well. Add the egg and mix well. Remove the heavy stem from the cabbage leaves. Place ⅓ of a cup of meat mixture on each cabbage leaf, and make 4 folds to form a sealed packet. Place cabbage rolls seam side down on the bed of cabbage. Add water to the pan, cover in foil, and bake in oven for 30 minutes. Remove casserole from oven and remove the foil. Drizzle ½ of the maple syrup on the cabbage rolls and place back in the oven uncovered for 30 minutes.

In a separate small pan add the cranberries, orange juice, corn syrup, zest, cinnamon, cardamon, and salt and pepper. Cook sauce for 10 minutes on medium heat.

Pull the cabbage casserole from the oven, drizzle it with the remaining maple syrup, and then bake for another 10 minutes. When ready to serve, place a portion of the chopped cabbage on the plate and top with a cabbage roll. Garnish with bacon and parsley. Serve with cranberry sauce and mashed or steamed potatoes.

REMMI NOTES: There are different versions of this recipe from all over the world. I was not sure about the syrup ingredient (which is an usual component of this dish when Finns prepare it), but ended up loving this dish. I think the sweet and sour flavors are a real treat. This dish is usually served with lingonberry sauce, but I substituted cranberries for lingonberries, as they just could not be found! Serve this dish with potatoes, as that's how they do it in Finland!

"It's not about what home cooks know; anyone can cook! It's about enjoying the fun of the creation!"

—Christos Athanasiadis

Going south from Finland and passing through the Gulf of Finland, we arrive at our next European adventure. Seven countries share a border with Poland, including Russia, Lithuania, Belarus, Slovakia, Ukraine, the Czech Republic, and Germany. The name "Poland" is derived from the title of a tribe called Polanie, which means "people living in open fields." Poles typically peel their bananas from the bottom. Poland is also the world's largest amber exporter. The Polish alphabet contains thirty-two letters, whereas the English language only uses twenty-six.

I selected pierogi to highlight as the food from this country, but there were many dishes that intrigued me. Their cuisine encompasses a lot of dishes I have tried and enjoy. I love stuffed cabbage rolls, potato pancakes with applesauce, and pyzy, which is another type of dumpling filled with meats. Meats, bread, and potatoes are the mainstays of the Polish diet.

CUCUMBER SALAD WITH YOGURT

INGREDIENTS:

2 medium cucumbers (scored and partially skinned, sliced thin— see directions)

1 shallot (sliced thin)

2 Tbsp. fresh dill

⅓ cup Greek yogurt (low fat)

1½ tsp. lemon juice

½ tsp. sugar

Salt and pepper to taste

DIRECTIONS:

Prepare all of the ingredients as directed. In a medium bowl, mix together all ingredients. Cover with plastic wrap and chill in refrigerator until ready to serve.

Note: To make a great presentation, peel the cucumber only partially. The skin of a cucumber contains fiber and is good for you! Using the tines of a fork, score the cucumber before slicing.

REMMI NOTES: This dish is incredibly simple to make, and you can have a super delectable salad within minutes! The dill really shines in this dish, and the lemon juice adds a refreshing factor.

PIEROGI WITH TOASTED WALNUTS

INGREDIENTS:

Dough: [See my notes]
2 cups flour
½ tsp. salt
1 egg
½ cup sour cream
¼ cup + 2 Tbsp. butter (divided;
   at room temperature)

Pierogi Filling:
1½ cup potatoes (boiled/mashed)
½ cup cheddar cheese (shredded)
1½ Tbsp. chives
Salt and pepper to taste
1 sweet onion (sliced in thin rounds)
½ cup walnuts (broken pieces/toasted)
¼ cup parsley (chopped)

DIRECTIONS:

Prepare ingredients as specified in ingredients lists, then prepare the dough as follows: In a medium bowl mix the flour and salt. Add egg and mix. Gradually add the sour cream and ¼ cup butter. Once mixed, gently fold and knead the dough until it is moist but not sticky. Place dough in plastic wrap and chill in the refrigerator for 30 minutes. In a small bowl mix potatoes, cheese, chives, and salt and pepper for filling.

Roll dough to ⅛" thickness. Use a 3"-wide glass to cut rounds. Place 2 tsp. of the filling mixture in the middle of the round and fold in half. Seal the pierogi with the tines of a fork. Place prepared pierogi on a baking sheet with wax or parchment paper on top so they do not dry out. In a small saucepan, melt the remaining butter and add the onions. Sauté until onions are golden.

Bring a large pot of salted water to a low boil. Add pierogi in batches as to not overcrowd them and stir occasionally to prevent sticking. They will sink to the bottom of the pan. Once they surface to the top, cook for 1-2 minutes longer. Test one to make sure they are cooked through.

When ready to serve, place the pierogi on a serving platter, top with the onion and butter mixture, and garnish with toasted walnuts and fresh parsley. Serve with the cucumber salad.

REMMI NOTES: This recipe for the dough is from King Arthur Flour, and it is a very simple dough recipe that fits this dish. There are various ways to make this type of dough; though some believe an egg is not good for dough, I experimented with several recipes and found this one performs the best for pierogi. Most often pierogi is served with sour cream. I added the cucumber salad with yogurt as a healthy alternative...and for its YUM factor!

Moving south from Poland and crossing the Ukraine, one reaches the beautiful country of Moldova. It is home to the world's largest collection of wine, containing over two million bottles! Winemaking here dates back at least 4,000 years. On National Wine Day, Moldovan wine producers open their vineyards to the public for wine tastings. It is considered impolite to enter someone's house wearing shoes, and slippers are offered by the host. The Moldovan village of Criva is home to one of the largest caves in the world. In 1991, Moldova gained independence from the U.S.S.R.

Moldovan cuisine is heavily influenced by Russian, Turkish, and Ukrainian cuisine. They use fruits and vegetables in a lot of their meals, because they have very rich soil which produces a variety of fresh produce. One of their staple dishes is mămăligă, a corn-based porridge of sorts. It is often served as a side that you can dress up or dress down, usually with meat-based entrées. One of their delicacies is a sheep's milk cheese called branza, which is often served alongside mămăligă.

POLENTA RATATOUILLE (MĂMĂLIGĂ)

Prep time: 25 minutes • Cook time: 1 hour

INGREDIENTS:

Ratatouille:

2 Tbsp. olive oil

2 garlic cloves (rough chop)

1 onion (1" slices)

1 green bell pepper (1" slices)

1 red bell pepper (1" slices)

1 eggplant (1½" cubes)

1 zucchini (½" 'half moon' slices)

1 yellow squash (½" 'half moon' slices)

6 oz. tomato sauce

½ tsp. dried sage

1½ cups cherry tomatoes

Salt and pepper to taste

2 Tbsp. fresh basil (chopped)

2 tsp. lemon zest

⅓ cup Parmesan cheese

Polenta:

4 cups water

1 cup coarse cornmeal

Salt to taste

Cooking spray

2 Tbsp. butter

DIRECTIONS:

Prepare all of the ingredients as directed. For the polenta, bring water to a boil and slowly add the cornmeal. Bring heat to low. Cook for 45 minutes, stirring every 10 minutes. Once the polenta is finished cooking, stir in the butter, and then salt to taste. Place the polenta in serving size-portions in small bowls, after spraying each bowl with cooking spray.

For the ratatouille, in a medium sauté pan, heat the oil, then add the onions and garlic and sauté for 1 minute. Add the bell peppers and eggplant and sauté for 5 minutes. Add the zucchini and yellow squash and sauté for 2 minutes. Add the tomato sauce and sage; then bring to a simmer and cook for 5 minutes, or until the eggplant and squashes are tender. Add the tomatoes and salt and pepper to taste. Cover the pan and remove from heat. When ready to serve, place polenta on individual plates. Top each serving with the vegetable ratatouille, and garnish with basil, zest, and parmesan. Note: This dish also plates beautifully when the polenta is packed into a small bowl or individual mold dish. Turn bowl/mold upside down on serving plate—polenta should slide out of the mold. Top each serving with the vegetable ratatouille and garnishes.

REMMI NOTES: Moldovan Mămăligă is not only fun to say but also fun to make! Mămăligă is the easy cornmeal base for this ratatouille dish. This dish has so much flavor yet only requires a little work. It is a hearty dish that should be paired with a lighter salad for a well-balanced meal. You can always add a little heat to the ratatouille by adding dried red pepper flakes for a bolder flavor!

Leaving Moldova, we cross central Europe through Romania and Serbia to reach our next destination. Croatia borders the Adriatic Sea; it is made up of 1,244 islands and reefs, but only forty-eight of them are inhabited. The Croatian city of Hum has a population of only twenty-five people, making it the smallest city in the world. Croatia's University of Zagreb was founded in 1669. The region of Dalmatia in Croatia is home to the Dalmatian dog breed made famous by Disney. A Croatian named Anthony Maglica is the inventor of the "Mag Lite" flashlight. The necktie originated in Croatia and was worn by Croatian soldiers. Fun facts!

Croatian cuisine has evolved over time along with its fascinating history. Many influences come from its neighbors: Hungary, Italy, and nearby Austria. On the coast, a lot of their dishes include seafood, due to their location on the Balkan Peninsula bordering the Adriatic Sea. Peka is a method of cooking foods over burning wood and is very popular in continental Croatia. Lunch is the largest meal of the day, and Croatians rarely eat at restaurants. They also love using seasonal fruits and vegetables. For example, punjeni artichoke is very popular in the spring, because that is when artichokes are in season. Stuffed bell peppers are another favorite when the peppers are in season. I read that most cooks have their own best way of making stuffed peppers, so there are many, many variations of this delicious recipe!

STUFFED ARTICHOKES (PUNJENI ARTICHOKE)

INGREDIENTS:

4 artichokes

1¼ cups fresh breadcrumbs

2 tsp. garlic (minced)

⅓ cup Italian parsley (chopped)

2 Tbsp. olive oil

Salt and pepper to taste

1 lemon (sliced)

1 Tbsp. tarragon (dried)

1 cup peas (frozen)

¼ cup lemon juice

¼ cup butter (melted)

DIRECTIONS:

Wash artichokes. Lay each artichoke on its side; with a sharp knife cut 1" off the top of the artichoke. Open the artichoke and remove the choke with a spoon. With a pair of scissors, snip the remaining pointed tips. Mix breadcrumbs, garlic, parsley, olive oil, and salt and pepper. Flatten each artichoke and stuff the center and leaves with the bread mixture. Place the artichokes in a stock pot and fill with water to the point where the artichokes are only half submerged. Add the lemon slices and 1 Tbsp. tarragon. Bring pot to a boil and reduce heat to low. Place a lid partialy on the stock pot. Cook for 45 minutes. Remove pot from heat and add the peas and place lid tightly on the pot. Prepare the dipping mixture by combining the lemon with the butter.

REMMI NOTES: I didn't know that artichokes got any better, until I discovered punjeni artichokes. The simple process of stuffing the artichokes not only makes them look delicious, but it enhances the overall flavor of the artichoke! I would be careful with the tarragon because it is a stronger spice and you don't want to overpower the dish. I love this stuffed version of these delicaces, but I just had to add the dipping sauce, not just for flavor, but also for the fun!

STUFFED BELL PEPPERS (PUNJENE PAPRIKE)

INGREDIENTS:

4 bell peppers

½ cup rice (parboiled for 3-4 minutes
  and drained)

1½ lb. ground chuck

½ cup onion (minced)

½ cup celery (small dice)

½ cup carrot (small dice)

2 garlic cloves (minced)

½ cup parsley (divided)

1 tsp. paprika

1½ Tbsp. beef bouillon granules

1 egg

Salt and pepper to taste

1-32 oz. can tomato juice

DIRECTIONS:

Wash bell peppers. Cut off the top and set aside. Remove seeds from the pepper. Parboil rice for 4-5 minutes and drain. In a large bowl, mix all of the remaining ingredients except the tomato. Fill the peppers with the meat and rice filling mixture. Place the peppers in a medium stock pot; then place the tops on the peppers. Pour tomato juice around the peppers. Add salt and pepper to the sauce if desired. Bring to a boil, and then turn down to a simmer and cover. Cook peppers for 50-60 minutes. If you desire a thicker sauce, you can add 2 Tbsp. of cornstarch diluted with water to the sauce. Serve in shallow heated bowls with mashed potatoes. Garnish with the remaining parsley.

REMMI NOTES: Stuffed peppers and mashed potatoes are over-the-top delicious...the taste of happiness.

From Croatia let's set sail southwards on the Adriatic Sea to Albania, passing the borders of Bosnia and Montenegro on the way. Albania is bordered by four other southern European countrie: Montenegro, Serbia, Macedonia, and Greece. It does not use the European euro as currency; their currency is the Albanian Lek. Albania is located on the Adriatic and Ionian Seas, with 300 miles of beautiful beaches. The one single Nobel Peace Prize winner to come from Albania so far is Mother Teresa.

Albanian cuisine is influenced by Balkan and Turkish influences. Albanians are known for their generosity and hospitality. If a guest is invited for dinner, Albanians will at times spend an entire month's salary to host them…now that's hospitality! Albanians love soups; I tested an Albanian recipe for "Lemon Chicken Soup," and it was a delightful standout.

MEATBALLS WITH YOGURT SAUCE (QOFTE)

Prep time: 20 minutes • Cook time: 15 minutes

INGREDIENTS:

Meatballs:
1½ lbs. ground beef
½ medium onion (small dice)
1 Tbsp. dried mint
½ cup dried bread crumbs
3 tsp. parsley (minced)
2 eggs
¼ cup feta cheese (crumbled)
Salt and pepper to taste
1 cup flour
2 Tbsp. olive oil
Fresh mint for garnish

Cucumber Mint Yogurt:
½ cup cucumber (small dice)
1½ cups plain yogurt
½ tsp. mint (finely chopped)
Pepper

DIRECTIONS:

Meatballs: Preheat oven to 350 degrees. Prepare all of the ingredients as specified in the ingredients list. Prepare a baking sheet by spraying with cooking oil or by placing a piece of parchment paper on the sheet. In a medium mixing bowl, combine all ingredients for the meatballs except the flour, olive oil, and fresh mint. Roll the meat to form 1½" meatballs. Place the flour on a plate or flat surface. Roll the qofte in the flour until lightly coated. Place the meatballs on baking sheet. Lightly drizzle olive oil over the meatballs. Cook in the oven for about 15 minutes or until fully cooked.

Cucumber Mint Yogurt: Prepare ingredients as directed. While the meatballs are cooking, mix all yogurt ingredients together in a small bowl and refrigerate until serving time.

REMMI NOTES: Be sure to pack your meatballs tightly when shaping them so that they hold together in the oven! The nutty flavor of the feta comes through in the meatballs and is complemented very well by the mint in the yogurt.

STUFFED PEPPERS WITH COTTAGE CHEESE

INGREDIENTS:

2 medium bell peppers (sliced through stem in halves, seeds removed)

1 Tbsp. olive oil

1/3 cup onion (chopped)

1 cup cottage cheese

2 eggs

1/4 tsp. cayenne pepper (optional)

8 oz. tomato sauce (divided)

1/4 cup basil (chopped)

Salt and pepper

1 tomato (sliced thick)

Chives (garnish)

DIRECTIONS:

Preheat oven to 375 degrees. Prepare all of the ingredients as specified in the ingredients list. Oil a small sauté pan with the olive oil and sauté the onions for 2-3 minutes. In a medium bowl, whisk the cottage cheese with the eggs, then add cayenne (if using), 4 oz. of the tomato sauce, basil, onion, salt, and pepper and mix. Place remaining tomato sauce in the baking pan. Evenly divide the cheese mixture into the pepper halves. Evenly divide the tomato slices and top each pepper. Place in the oven for 40 minutes. Remove from the oven and garnish with chives.

REMMI NOTES: These stuffed peppers may seem a little unconventional with the cottage cheese, but the flavors inside the pepper, like the onion and the basil, really shine to make this a delicious and unique treat!

SAFFRON RICE PILAF

INGREDIENTS:

1½ Tbsp. olive oil
1½ cups rice (medium-long grain)
3 cups chicken broth

Pinch of saffron
Salt and pepper to taste

DIRECTIONS:

Add olive oil to a medium sauce pan. Add the rice to the pan and briefly sauté for 1 minute. Add chicken broth and saffron to the pan and bring to a boil over high heat. Once boiling, decrease heat to low and cover. Cook for about 15 minutes or until rice is tender.

OR...you can serve Stuffed Peppers with Cottage Cheese as your main entrée with the saffron rice. I so love stuffed peppers, and they are an important part of the cuisine in this region. This is a meatless yet very filling, mellow, and scrumptious dish!

REMMI NOTES: Meatballs come in all shapes, sizes, and cuisines! Usually Albanian meatballs or qoftes have feta cheese in them. I like to combine the rice with the mint yogurt and then a little bit of meatball, all together in one bite! The flavors blend so well! If you don't have saffron, you can always substitute a pinch of turmeric that will still make the rice pop with color. Plate rice first, adding meatballs on top and then a dollop or two of yogurt on the side. YUM!

Crossing the Albanian border, we travel next to Greece. Greeks call their country Hellas or Ellada, but its official name is the Hellenistic Republic. Instead of having a grand celebration for someone's birthday, they have a celebration for their "Name Day." In the Orthodox Church, every day is dedicated to a saint, and if you're named after one, then there is quite a large gathering with family and friends. If you are eighteen years old, it is against the law for a Greek citizen not to vote. Greece is made up of 3,000 islands, but only 170 are inhabited.

Greek cuisine is filled with fresh, flavorful dishes. The ancient Greek writer Archestratus wrote the first cookbook in 330 BC and he wrote about how to find good food in the Mediterranean. The tradition of chefs wearing tall white hats originated with the Greeks. Grapes, olives, and grains are a mainstay of their daily diets, and olive oil goes into just about every dish they make.

GREEK SALAD

INGREDIENTS:

1 cucumber (¼" "half moon" slices)

1 cup cherry tomatoes (sliced in half)

1 bell pepper (¼" strips)

¾ cup Kalamata olives (drained)

¼ cup red Onion (sliced thin)

½ cup feta cheese (crumbled)

¼ cup olive oil

2 Tbsp. red wine vinegar

2 Tbsp. lemon juice

1 garlic (crushed)

½ tsp. sugar

⅓ cup parsley (chopped)

DIRECTIONS:

Prepare all of the ingredients as directed. In a medium bowl place cucumber, tomatoes, bell pepper, olives, onion, and feta cheese. In a small bowl, mix the remaining ingredients. When ready to serve, toss the salad with the dressing.

REMMI NOTES: Greek salad takes a little bit of work to prepare, but once all of the chopping is done, it is super easy to put together! Feta cheese adds just the amount of saltiness that this salad needs as well as halps to tame the red onion's bite. The garlic in the dressing adds a stronger flavor to the more subtle ingredients, like the cucumber and bell pepper.

MEAT AND VEGETABLE CASSEROLE (MOUSSAKA)

INGREDIENTS:

4 Tbsp. olive oil (divided)

2 large eggplants (½" rounds)

2 large potatoes (peeled and sliced in ¼"
  rounds)

Meat Sauce:

2 Tbsp. olive oil

1½ lb. ground lamb or beef

1 cup onions (diced)

2 garlic (minced)

1 14 oz. can diced tomatoes

1 Tbsp. lemon juice

½ tsp. ground cinnamon

⅛ tsp. nutmeg

1 cup beef or vegetable broth

2½ Tbsp. tomato paste

⅓ cup parsley (chopped)

Béchamel Sauce:

3 cups milk

3 Tbsp. butter

3 Tbsp. flour

¼ tsp. nutmeg

Salt and pepper

2 egg yolks

2 tsp. lemon zest

1 cup Pecorino Romano cheese (grated
  and divided)

Parsley (chopped, as garnish)

DIRECTIONS:

Preheat oven to 400 degrees. Prepare all of the ingredients as specified in ingredients lists. Place eggplant rounds on paper towels, and salt generously. Let stand for 30 minutes, then rinse and pat dry. Place eggplant rounds on a baking sheet and drizzle with 2 Tbsp. olive oil. Bake in oven for 20 minutes or until tender. Place the potato rounds on a baking sheet and drizzle with 1 Tbsp. olive oil. Bake in oven for 10 minutes or until tender.

In a medium pan, heat 1 Tbsp. olive oil and add the lamb or beef with the onions and garlic. Sauté until the meat is cooked. Drain any grease from the pan. Add the remaining meat sauce ingredients. Bring to a boil and then turn the heat to simmer and cook for 20 minutes.

To prepare béchamel sauce, in a small pan, scald the milk. In a small saucepan, heat the butter, and then add the flour and whisk to make a smooth roux. Lower heat and gradually add the scalded milk using a whisk. Once the sauce starts to thicken, cook for 1–2 minutes longer. Add a couple of Tbsp.s of sauce to the egg yolks to temper, and then add to the sauce. Remove from heat and add the nutmeg, salt, pepper, lemon zest, and ⅓ cup of cheese.

To assemble, lightly spray a three-quart oven dish with cooking oil. First layer the potatoes, then top with a layer of half of the eggplant and ⅓ cup of cheese. Next cover with the meat sauce and then the final layer of remaining eggplant and remaining ⅓ cup of cheese. Pour the bechamel sauce on the casserole and smooth it with the back of a spoon. Place in oven for 30– 40 minutes until it is bubbly and the crust is golden. Allow to rest for 20 minutes and garnish with parsley when serving.

REMMI NOTES: Béchamel sauce is one of the five "Grand Sauces," and it is understood that when once learned, a cook becomes a chef! Béchamel is creamy, smooth, and sophisticated and can turn any dish into something extra special and memorable. That is exactly what the béchamel sauce brings to this dish. It is a bit complex to create, but it is worth the effort. Love it!

Due west of Greece across the Mediterranean Sea we find one of my all-time favorite cuisines. Spain is in the Iberian Peninsula; it has two large archipelagos, the Baltic and the Canary Islands. It is the only European country to border an African country (Morocco). Uniquely, Spain also has two "autonomous" cities, Ceuta and Melilla, which are Spanish possessions even though they are in North Africa. Spain is rich with unique customs and traditions. Lunch is the most important meal of the day, and it is usually served between 2:00 and 4:00 p.m. Dinner is a smaller meal usually served at 10:00 p.m. Over half of the world's olive oil is produced in Spain. Tourism in Spain is major, since fully as many foreigners visit the country in a one-year period as there are residents living there.

Paella, which originated in Valencia in eastern Spain, is the highly regarded national dish. It began as an easy lunch for farmers or workers, who started with a rice base and added what was available, such as rabbit, snails, and green and white beans. Even though women traditionally do the cooking, it is customary for men to cook the paella. There are paella competitions all over the country, and it usually served at big gatherings of family and friends. The dish has evolved and there are now many varieties of paella—this is one take on it, but you can always add your own touches!

SEAFOOD PAELLA

INGREDIENTS:

2 Tbsp. olive oil plus additional as needed

¼ cup flour

1 Tbsp. paprika

1 whole chicken (cut into 10 pieces)

2 Italian sausage links

1 cup onion (small dice)

1 cup carrots (medium dice)

½ cup celery (medium dice)

1½ lb. shrimp [See my notes]

2 lobster tails [See my notes]

4 cups rice

1-14.5 oz. can diced tomatoes (undrained)

5½ cups chicken stock (or vegetable stock)

½ tsp. saffron

Salt and pepper

1 cup frozen peas

¼ cup parsley (garnish)

1 lemon (sliced in wedges for garnish)

DIRECTIONS:

Prepare all of the ingredients as specified in the ingredients list. Mix the flour and paprika and lightly dust the chicken pieces. Salt and pepper the chicken. Add olive oil to a deep frying pan. Sear the chicken in the oil until lightly browned. Remove the chicken and set aside. Add the Italian sausages and brown. Remove sausages from pan and slice horizontally in 1½" pieces. Sauté shrimp and lobster for 2 minutes, then remove from pan. Add the onions, carrots, and celery, and sauté for 3 minutes. (You may need to add additional olive oil.)

Add the rice to the vegetables and sauté for 2 minutes. Add the tomatoes and chicken broth and bring to a boil. Add saffron and salt and pepper and turn heat to medium high. Cook the rice, stirring occasionally for 10 minutes. Add the chicken and sausage by tucking the meat under the rice. Place paella in an oven preheated to 325 degrees for 20 minutes. Take the paella out of the oven and add the lobster tails, shrimp, and peas. Cover pan with a lid or foil and let it sit for 15-20 minutes to finish the cooking. Garnish with the parsley and limes.

Note: You can use any combination of 5 cups of seafood. If using clams or mussels, add those to the rice mixture just before placing the paella in the oven.

REMMI NOTES: A couple of the main reasons I love paella are because it is so customizable and I love rice! I enjoy this version, because I usually don't get to eat a lot of seafood in the Midwest, but when we make paella it is always a nice treat! You can choose one type of meat or protein or you can mix and match, like in this recipe. Saffron can be slightly expensive, so if you wanted a substitute, you can add turmeric in order to keep that yellow hue; just add it at the same time the saffron would have been added. This recipe serves eight, and you can cut the ingredients in half and serve the half-recipe as appetizer or tapas portions. Although it isn't customary and this dish really doesn't exactly need it, sometimes I like to pair this with plain yogurt as a side, which gives it a very creamy texture!

"I don't like gourmet cooking or 'this' cooking or 'that' cooking. I like good cooking."

—James Beard

CONTINENT OF AFRICA

"Cooking is like painting or writing a song. Just as there are only so many notes or colors, there are only so many flavors. It's how you combine them that sets you apart."
—**Wolfgang Puck**

The continent of Africa has the second largest population on earth and the second largest land mass. The continent is surrounded by five bodies of water: the Indian Ocean, the Atlantic Ocean, the Mediterranean Sea, the Suez Canal, and the Red Sea. It is considered the continent first inhabited by humans. Africa is rich in many minerals and natural resources, with 90 percent of the world's cobalt, 50 percent of the world's gold, and 98 percent of the world's chromium (a trace element necessary for human health), to name a few.

From the southern tip of Spain, we cross the Strait of Gibraltar to our new continent. Morocco is in the northwest corner of Africa across from Spain. It is bordered by the North Atlantic Ocean and the Mediterranean Sea. Morocco is officially known as the Kingdom of Morocco. Morocco is a country with a rich culture and is known to have some of the friendliest people in the world. It is filled with beautiful natural landscapes and breathtaking architecture, and its capital is Rabat. The largest city in Morocco is Casablanca. Moroccans enjoy sipping mint tea sweetened with sugar while visiting with family and guests.

Moroccan cuisine is rich and often filled with an abundance of flavorful spices. Moroccan cuisine uses fruits such as apples and dates to bring sweetness to savory dishes. Cumin is their spice of choice, and it is often on the table ready to use just like salt and pepper. Flavored waters like orange blossom and rose water are added to desserts and salads for a uniquely delectable depth. Couscous is an important staple in Morocco. Salads are often combinations of fruits with vegetables, and dessert is usually a simple dish of fruit dusted with spices. Try oranges with cinnamon for a simple but refreshing dessert. The main meal in Morocco is often served midday; it starts with a salad followed by the traditional meal, with some tea with mint at the end. A classic Moroccan meal is Moroccan Chicken Tagine, which is a chicken dish prepared in a Dutch oven or any heavy cooking pot.

MOROCCAN ORANGE SALAD

Prep time: 15 minutes

INGREDIENTS:

3 cups romaine lettuce (sliced 1" strips)

2 oranges (peeled ½" slices)

2 Tbsp. pistachios (toasted)

4 Tbsp. orange juice

2 Tbsp. vinegar

1½ tsp. honey

¼ tsp. cinnamon

¼ tsp. cumin

½ tsp. orange zest

Salt and pepper to taste

Fresh parsley (garnish)

DIRECTIONS:

Prepare all of the ingredients as specified in the ingredients list. On a medium platter, layer the lettuce, oranges, and pistachios. Mix remaining ingredients. When ready to serve, drizzle dressing on the salad. Garnish with parsley.

REMMI NOTES: I love to use citrus in many of my dishes. This is one of my favorite salads because it highlights the orange—the nuttiness of the pistachios helps balance the sweetness of the flavor, and they add another crunchy component to the dish, along with the romaine!

CHICKEN TAGINE WITH LEMON COUSCOUS AND YOGURT

Prep time: 25 minutes • Cook time: 1 hour 20 minutes

INGREDIENTS:

2–3 Tbsp. olive oil

4 chicken thighs and drumsticks (salted and peppered)

1 large onion (sliced)

3 cloves garlic (crushed)

½ tsp. cinnamon

½ tsp. turmeric

½ tsp. coriander

½ tsp. cumin

¼ tsp. cayenne pepper

Pinch of saffron (optional, but it really adds to the dish)

1–28 oz. can tomatoes (diced)

2 cups chicken broth

3 cups butternut squash (peeled, 1" dice)

1 cup dried apricots (quartered)

Salt and pepper to taste

3 cups baby spinach (washed)

2 cups plain couscous

½ cup plain yogurt

Parsley for garnish

DIRECTIONS:

Make the couscous according to the package directions, adding 1 Tbsp. of lemon juice and the zest of half a lemon. Prepare all other ingredients as specified in the ingredients list. Preheat oven to 350 degrees. In a Dutch oven, brown the chicken pieces in olive oil for 4 minutes on each side. Remove from Dutch oven and set aside. Add the onion slices and garlic to the pan and sauté for 2 minutes. Add the cinnamon, turmeric, coriander, cumin, cayenne, and saffron. Stir to blend and add the tomatoes, chicken stock, and squash. Bring to a boil and reduce heat to a simmer for 10 minutes. Salt and pepper to taste. Add the apricots. Place the chicken on top of the squash mixture. The chicken should be partially submerged in the liquid. Cover the Dutch oven with a lid or foil, and place in the oven for 1 hour. Remove from oven and add the spinach. To serve, divide the couscous among four bowls and top with a serving of the tagine. Garnish with yogurt and parsley.

REMMI NOTES: I know the tagine looks like a detailed recipe, but it isn't complicated. It is only a two-step process of browning the chicken and then combining the rest of the ingredients into one pot before you put it in the oven. Tagines can be made from many different kinds of meats as well as fish. What makes this dish so enjoyable is the combination of great spices in the dish. I also added the apricots to add a subtle, natural sweetness to the dish. As I always say, experiment away with all kinds of sweet or savory additions to make it your own, but just make sure to constantly taste to make sure it's delicious!

From Morocco, we travel from the northwest to the far northeast of Africa. Egypt is a country spanning the continents of Africa and Asia. The Sinai Peninsula part of Egypt is located in Asia; it is the landmass that connects Africa to Asia. The pyramid complex at Giza, located just outside of Cairo, is the oldest ancient wonder of the world that still exists, and it remains a renowned tourist attraction. The history behind the construction, purpose, and meaning of the pyramids is vast, fascinating, and complicated.

The cuisine of Egypt involves fruits, vegetables, and legumes, and closely fits the Mediterranean dietary profile. Pita bread is a mainstay at every meal. Baking at high heat causes the pita to puff in size; when cooled, the dough remains separated inside, which forms pockets. These bread pockets are great fun, as you can stuff them with fillings like salads and rice dishes. The national dish, kushari, is a mixture of macaroni, rice, and lentils. Pasta, rice, and beans all in one dish! Yes...that's heaven!

KUSHARI (EGYPTIAN RICE, LENTILS, AND MACARONI)

INGREDIENTS:

1½ cups uncooked white rice (prepare as directed)

1 cup uncooked lentils (prepare as directed)

1½ cups uncooked elbow macaroni (prepare as directed)

3 Tbsp. extra virgin olive oil

3 medium onions (2 onions sliced, 1 onion medium dice)

3 cloves garlic (minced)

2-14 oz. cans diced tomatoes

1 tsp. cumin

¾ tsp. coriander

¾ tsp. cinnamon

½ tsp. nutmeg

¼ tsp. crushed red pepper (or more to taste)

Salt and pepper to taste

4 Tbsp. fresh mint (chiffonade)

1½ tsp. lemon juice

1½ cups plain yogurt

1-14 oz. can garbanzo beans (optional; washed and drained)

DIRECTIONS:

Prepare all of the ingredients as specified in the ingredients list. Prepare the rice and set aside. Prepare the lentils and pasta (separately) following package directions. Drain the pasta and the lentils when fully cooked.

In a medium saucepan, add the olive oil and the sliced onions; the slices should be separated into rings. Cook over medium high heat until the onions are crunchy. Place the cooked onions on a paper towel. Using the same pan to cook the onions, add the diced onions to the pan. Sauté the onions for 1-2 minutes, and then add the garlic and sauté for 1 minute. Add the diced tomatoes, cumin, coriander, cinnamon, nutmeg, and crushed red pepper, and salt and pepper to taste. Bring the tomato sauce to a boil, and then reduce heat and simmer for 15 minutes.

In a small bowl, mix yogurt, 2 Tbsp. mint, and lemon juice well. To serve, layer ingredients on a large platter or in individual bowls in the following order: rice, pasta, lentils, tomato sauce, garbanzo beans (if using), and cooked onions. Garnish with remaining mint and serve with the yogurt sauce on the side.

REMMI NOTES: In my research, I learned that this dish is a popular street food and is served in every home and restaurant. When I saw the combination of pasta, lentils, and macaroni, I just had to go for it! There are hundreds of kushari recipes using different spice combinations. While I included the garbanzo beans just as an optional garnish (since they're not one of my favorites), in Egypt, they are usually used in this dish. I am an enthusiast of yogurt, and I never, ever eat a rice dish without either a side of plain yogurt or a yogurt sauce. You should try it with kushari, because it adds great flavor to this spicy dish! Often this dish is served with all of the ingredients just mixed together, but it presents beautifully when plated in layers as suggested.

Leaving Egypt and traveling through Chad, we come to our next stop on the west coast of Africa. Nigeria is Africa's most populous country, and it also has the largest population of youth in the world. Nigeria is known as the "Giant of Africa" because of its large population. It is very diverse—at least 250 different languages are spoken. Their oil industry, the largest in Africa, is a major aspect of the Nigerian economy. Soccer is a very popular sport in Nigeria. A staple fruit that can be found in almost all Nigerian grocery stores is the plantain. One popular Nigerian dish is fried plantain, which is called "dodo."

Nigeria has a vast culture with amazing cuisine. With its variety of spices and different local ingredients, the aromas of Nigerian cuisine are quite amazing. Trade played a major role in the evolution of African cuisine. The original staple foods of Nigeria were rice, millet, and lentils. In the fifteenth century, Portuguese explorers and traders established a slave trade center in Nigeria. Later on, several other countries tried to gain control of the slave trade in Nigeria. European traders introduced many other staples including beans, cassava, and maize. Other foods that were introduced were spices such as pepper, cinnamon, and nutmeg, which are still used in African cuisine today. Because Nigeria is a mostly tropical region, many fruits, including oranges, melons, grapefruit, limes, mangoes, bananas, and pineapple are enjoyed year-round.

JOLLOF RICE WITH CHICKEN

INGREDIENTS:

Chicken:

1½ lbs. chicken legs (you can substitute chicken thighs)

1½ tsp. salt

1½ tsp. onion powder

1½ tsp. garlic powder

1½ tsp. paprika

½ tsp. cayenne pepper

¾ tsp. chicken bouillon powder

Rice:

1 onion (medium dice)

3 cloves garlic (minced)

2 cups long grain rice (uncooked)

1 cup tomato sauce

3 cups chicken stock

1 tsp. chicken bouillon powder

1 tsp. salt

1 tsp. paprika

1 tsp. pepper

1 tsp. cayenne pepper (optional, to add a little heat)

1 cup vegetables (sliced in bite size pieces—I used carrots and cauliflower)

DIRECTIONS:

Chicken: Prepare ingredients as directed. In a small bowl, mix spices together and dust each chicken piece with the chicken spices. Add 2 Tbsp. of olive oil to a large skillet. Brown both sides of the chicken over medium-high heat, about 3-4 minutes on each side. Once chicken is golden, remove from the pan and set aside.

Rice: In a large bowl, cover rice with cold water and wash grains. Pour out water and repeat until the water becomes clear. Remove any excess oil from the skillet used to cook the chicken, then add a couple Tbsp. of olive oil to the pan. Sauté onion and garlic over medium-high heat until soft, about 2 minutes. Then stir in rice and let sauté for an additional minute. Pour in tomato sauce, chicken stock, and remaining spices. Gently stir to combine. Add chicken and bring to a boil. Cover pan and place in the oven at 350 degrees for about 15-20 minutes, then add the vegetables on top and cook for another 10-15 minutes or until rice is fully cooked. (Note: Be careful of the rice getting too dry. If it does, you can add some more chicken stock to moisten it.) Remove from the oven and let cool for about 5 minutes. Serve warm and enjoy!

REMMI NOTES: This is a great one-pan meal that's very affordable. Fresh fruit or a fresh salad would go great with this dish. In Nigeria, you would most likely be served this dish with dodo, which is fried plantains. Yum!

"Cooking is so popular today because it's the perfect mix of food and fun."

—Emeril Lagasse

Traversing Africa once again, we leave its western coastal region and cross over to the southern hemisphere zone on the east coast. Tanzania is a country in East Africa, bordering the Indian Ocean. Tanzania is full of wildlife like elephants, zebras, lions, crocodiles, and chimpanzees. It is also known for its beautiful beaches and friendly locals. Tanzania is home to the highest peak in Africa, Mount Kilimanjaro, which was once an active volcano. The Serengeti National Park is the oldest and most popular park to tour in Tanzania—it is home to 1.7 million wild beasts. Soccer is the favored sport in this country. Tanzania is the world's largest producer of cloves.

There are over 120 different tribes in Tanzania, and they are known for their courtesy and tolerance. Elders are greatly respected. The official Tanzanian language is Swahili, but almost everyone speaks English. Ugali is the national food—it is a cornmeal mush that is rolled in a ball and used in eating other food. Food is served on communal platters, and it is considered improper to eat with your left hand. If you are a guest at a private home in Tanzania, be prepared to eat well, as it is rude to refuse food. One interesting fact is that the cook is highly respected and sits at the head of the table.

TANZANIAN FAMILY FEAST

NYAMA CHOMA (GRILLED MEAT)

Prep time: 10 minutes • Cook time: 20 minutes

INGREDIENTS:

2 lbs. beef short ribs

2 Tbsp. oil

2 Tbsp. lemon juice

½ Tbsp. turmeric

2 cloves garlic (crushed)

DIRECTIONS:

Mix the oil, lemon juice, turmeric, and garlic to make the marinade. Place the meat in a glass bowl and pour in the marinade. The meat should marinate for at least an hour before roasting. Roast the meat on a grill until cooked.

PILAU (RICE)

INGREDIENTS:

2 Tbsp. oil

1 medium onion (small dice)

1½ cup basmati rice

¼ tsp. cloves

¼ tsp. cinnamon

½ tsp. cardamon

1 tsp. cumin

1 tsp. coriander

½ cup coconut milk

2½ cups chicken broth

Salt and pepper to taste

½ cup raisins

½ cup cashews

½ cup cilantro

DIRECTIONS:

Chop the onion to a small dice size. In a medium pan with a lid, sauté the rice and onions for 3 minutes. In a small bowl, mix the dry spice ingredients, and then combine with the rice mixture. Add the milk, chicken broth, and salt and pepper. Bring the rice to a boil, then reduce heat to low, cover, and cook for 20 minutes. Mix the raisins with the rice mixture. When ready to serve, place in a serving bowl and garnish with cashews and cilantro.

SALAD YA MATUNDA (FRUIT SALAD)

INGREDIENTS:

1 cup mango (large dice)

1 cup banana (large dice)

1 cup pineapple (large dice)

1 cup kiwi (large dice)

1 avocado (large dice)

2 Tbsp. orange juice

1 Tbsp. lime juice

2 Tbsp. fresh coconut

DIRECTIONS:

Chop all the fruit and avocado to a large dice size. Place the fruits in a medium bowl and toss with the orange and lime juices. Garnish with coconut.

KACHUMBARI (CABBAGE SALAD)

INGREDIENTS:

4 cups cabbage (thin sliced)

1 medium onion (thin sliced)

2 tomatoes (medium dice)

1 hot pepper (optional; seeded
   and minced)

Salt and pepper to taste

2 Tbsp. lime juice

1 Tbsp. oil

DIRECTIONS:

Prepare all of the ingredients as specified in the ingredients list. In a medium bowl, mix all ingredients with the oil and lime juice.

UGALI

INGREDIENTS:

2 cups water

1½ to 2 cups cornmeal (white cornmeal
  is traditional, but yellow will work)

DIRECTIONS:

Bring the water to a boil in a saucepan large enough to leave plenty of space when water is in it, then add cornmeal, stirring to prevent the formation of lumps. Continue slowly adding cornmeal until the resulting porridge is thick. Cook on medium-low heat while continuing to stir the ugali until the cornmeal is well cooked and smashing any lumps. When tipped into a dish, the finished ugali should hold its shape. Ugali is best served hot.

MCHUZI WA BIRINGANI (EGGPLANT AND POTATOES)

Prep time: 10 minutes • Cook time: 30 minutes

INGREDIENTS:

2 Tbsp. oil

1 large eggplant (large dice)

1 large onion (small dice)

2 medium sweet potatoes (peeled, large dice)

1–28 oz. can crushed tomatoes

1 cup water

1½ tsp. curry powder

¼ tsp. chili powder

¼ tsp. cinnamon

Salt and pepper to taste

DIRECTIONS:

Prepare the vegetables as specified in the ingredients list. In a medium pan, sauté the onion, eggplant, and sweet potatoes for 3 minutes. Add the remaining ingredients and simmer until all the vegetables are tender and the sauce has thickened (30 minutes). Serve with Ugali.

REMMI NOTE: Pilau is usually only served on special occasions, but at festive meals, it is served in every home. Adding raisins and cashews makes the dish special and gives it a sweet and crunchy bite. Fruits are abundant in Tanzania and are served in salads and desserts. Try different combinations of fruits for this dish. Ugali is the national dish, and it is served with stews and curries. You can easily find a recipe because it's a simple starch made from two parts water and one part cornmeal. Tanzanians use this food to scoop up sauces and gravies…with their fingers, so have a napkin nearby! Enjoy this Tanzanian family feast.

Moving to the south border of Tanzania, we arrive in Mozambique, a country in southeast Africa. It stretches for miles along Africa's southeast coast and features islands and amazing coral reefs with over 1,200 species of fish. Mozambique also contains a vast desert plateau with a tropical climate suitable for growing tropical fruits. Much of the population lives along Mozambique's coasts and rivers. Its capital is Maputo, the largest city in Mozambique, which features beautiful white sandy beaches.

Mozambique is widely known across Africa for its amazingly flavorful and colorful cuisine. The Portuguese have heavily influenced Mozambique cuisine, due to the many immigrants to Mozambique from Portugal. Mozambican cuisine can be *peri-peri*, meaning "spicy-spicy," because of the heavy use of chili pepper, garlic, and lemon, which are part of the Portuguese influence. In Mozambique, the hotter the better—sounds good to me! For those who live farther inland, maize porridge and meat and vegetable stew are staple foods. Since much of the population lives on the coast, fresh seafood is a large part of everyday meals. Shrimp Mozambique is a popular dish there that is quick to prepare.

SHRIMP MOZAMBIQUE

INGREDIENTS:

2 lbs. large shrimp (washed, peeled, and deveined)

Salt and pepper

4 Tbsp. flour

3 Tbsp. olive oil

4 Tbsp. butter (divided)

1 onion (small dice)

3 cloves garlic (minced)

1 beer

1 Tbsp. lemon juice

1 tsp. turmeric

½ tsp. saffron

¼ tsp. crushed red pepper (or more to taste)

1 large tomato (medium dice)

⅓ cup parsley (sliced)

1 lemon (sliced)

3 cups cooked rice

DIRECTIONS:

Prepare all of the ingredients as specified in the ingredients list. Salt and pepper shrimp and dredge in flour. Add the oil and 3 Tbsp. of butter to a medium sauce pan. Sauté the shrimp in the oil/butter mixture over medium high heat for 1 minute on each side. Remove the shrimp from the pan and set aside. Sauté onion and garlic in the same pan for 2 minutes. Add beer, lemon juice, turmeric, saffron, and crushed red pepper, and simmer for 5 minutes until thickened. Add tomato and shrimp to sauce to warm. Place rice on a platter, top with the shrimp mixture, and garnish with parsley and sliced lemons.

REMMI NOTES: Mozambique is one of the final countries I am covering in Africa. I am so delighted to include this recipe, as it is simpler than many of the recipes from other African countries. It's easy, and delicious. Enjoy!

From Mozambique, we cross the sea to a beautiful island to the east in the Indian Ocean. Madagascar is the fourth largest island in the world. Ninety percent of its plants and wildlife are not found anywhere else in the world. Fifty percent of the sapphires in the world are from Madagascar. Some of the finest tropical fruits, such as coconuts, mangos, pineapples, passion fruit, lychees, and persimmons are grown here. Garlic, onions, ginger, and curry are the main spices of the island's cuisine.

Maybe it is my Chinese heritage, but I love rice, and rice is served at every meal in Madagascar, breakfast, lunch, and dinner. For lunch and dinner, it is served with *laoka* as a side dish, which is a broth soup cooked with vegetables and meats. The main source of beef on the island is the Zebu cow. The kitchens of Madagascar are usually separate from the house for safety reasons, as food is cooked on an open fire in most homes; however, new solar stoves are being introduced. *Romazava* is the national dish; it is a stew of meats and greens. It is served with rice, of course!

VANILLA BEAN FRUIT SALAD

INGREDIENTS:

2 cups strawberries (sliced in half)

2 plums (cubed medium)

1 mango (two if small; cubed medium)

1 vanilla bean (seeds only)

2 Tbsp. fresh coconut

3 Tbsp. orange juice

1 Tbsp. lime juice

1 Tbsp. honey

Fresh mint

DIRECTIONS:

Prepare all of the ingredients as directed. Place the fruit in medium bowl. Scrape the seeds from the vanilla bean onto the fruit. Mix the orange juice, lime juice, and honey together. Toss with the fruits. Garnish with fresh mint.

ROMAZAVA (MADAGASCAR BEEF AND GREENS STEW)

Prep time: 15 minutes • Cook time: 30 minutes

INGREDIENTS:

2 Tbsp. olive oil

1 lb. beef stew meat

1 medium onion (small dice)

¾ cup celery (large dice)

2 cloves garlic (crushed)

2 cups beef broth

1 cup water

1-14 oz. can diced tomatoes

¼ tsp. crushed red pepper

Salt and pepper

8 cups leafy greens (collard or mustard greens, kale, or combination)

DIRECTIONS:

In medium pan, sauté the beef and onions in olive oil until the meat is browned. Add the celery, garlic, broth, water, tomatoes, crushed red pepper, and salt and pepper to taste. Add water if needed to cover the meat. Bring the pot to a boil, then reduce heat and simmer for 30 minutes. Add the leafy greens to the pot, cover, and remove from heat. Serve with steamed rice in heated bowls. Serve the Vanilla Bean Fruit Salad either with the stew or after, as fruit dishes are often served as desserts.

REMMI NOTE: Madagascar is another country that has so many exotic fruits. Also, this country produces 60 percent of the world's vanilla beans, so they are used a lot in their cooking. I know the fruit salad is very simple, but just wait and see how the vanilla bean makes this dish. The stew is a very versatile dish, because you can make it with different kinds of meat, like chicken or pork. Some recipes even feature a combination of meats. While I didn't use it in this stew recipe, ginger is a common ingredient in Romazava. It is one of those dishes that's fun to experiment with using different meats, vegetables, and seasoning!

Returning to the African mainland, the southernmost country is South Africa, which borders on both the Indian and the South Atlantic Ocean. South Africa has eleven official languages and three capital cities: Pretoria, Cape Town, and Bloemfontein. The most popular sports are "football" (soccer), rugby, and cricket. South Africa is home to two Nobel Prize winners: Nelson Mandela and Archbishop Desmond Tutu. South Africa is also the second-largest fruit producer in the world.

South Africa's colorful and vibrant cuisine has been influenced by its immigrant cultures, Holland, France, India, and Malaysia. "Bunny Chow," also known as "Bunnies," is a dish from the streets of Durban that has made its way through South Africa. Although it may sound like a bunny dish, no bunnies are harmed in the making of bunny chow. It is popular and easy to prepare, since it is made out of a hollowed loaf of bread stuffed with spicy curry. The spicy curry may be accompanied with meat, although the original dish was vegetarian.

BUNNY CHOW (CHICKEN CURRY BREAD BOWL)

Prep time: 15 minutes • Cook time: 35 minutes

INGREDIENTS:

2 Tbsp. oil

1 large onion (diced)

2 cloves garlic (minced)

1-28 oz. can crushed tomatoes

1 bay leaf

2 tsp. curry powder

1 tsp. cumin

1 tsp. turmeric.

1 tsp. coriander

¼ tsp. cayenne pepper

2 boneless/skinless chicken breasts (1"
cubes)

2 potatoes (1" dice)

2 large carrots (1" dice)

2 cups chicken broth

2 fresh tomatoes (medium dice)

½ cup peas

Salt and pepper to taste

Lime zest for garnish

Parsley for garnish

1 unsliced loaf of bread (square crusty
bread; cut in fourths and hollow to
make bowls)

DIRECTIONS:

Prepare all of the ingredients as specified in ingredient list. In a medium stockpot, sauté the onion and garlic in oil for 2 minutes. Add the can of tomatoes, bay leaf, curry, cumin, turmeric, coriander, cayenne pepper, chicken, potatoes, carrots, and chicken broth. Bring to a boil and simmer for 30 minutes partially covered with a lid. Check potatoes to make sure they are tender, and then add the fresh tomatoes and peas. Remove lid. Cook for an additional 5 minutes. Serve in individual bread bowls and garnish with lime zest and fresh parsley.

REMMI NOTES: Since this is such a spice-heavy dish, it's really important to adjust the seasonings to your taste. Add additional water to the Bunny Chow for a better texture if needed. Experiment with different flavors for this dish by substituting or adding different vegetables, such as cauliflower and sweet potatoes.

CARROT SAMBAL

Prep time: 15 minutes

INGREDIENTS:

4 large carrots (shredded)

¾ cup pineapple (fresh or canned, medium dice)

½ cup cucumber (medium dice)

¼ cup orange juice

1 Tbsp. lime juice

1 Tbsp. honey

¼ tsp. crushed red pepper

¼ tsp. nutmeg

Salt and pepper to taste

Mint leaves for garnish

DIRECTIONS:

Prepare all of the ingredients as directed. Mix the ingredients in a medium bowl, garnish with mint, and serve as a side with the Bunny Chow.

REMMI NOTES: The Carrot Sambal is a sweet but savory dish that complements the Bunny Chow. This is a great dish to experiment with using different fruits to accompany the sweet carrots. When it's time to devour the bunny chow dish, have some fun, since you are encouraged to eat with your fingers!

"Explore more and have more fun in the kitchen! Cook anything—just kick back and enjoy it!"

—Nina Compton

CONTINENT OF
ASIA

"This is my advice to people: learn how to cook, try new recipes, learn from your mistakes, be fearless, and above all have fun!"

—Julia Child

The Continent of Asia is the largest on the planet, both in area and population. It is home to forty-eight countries, including its most populous, China, which is where I was born! Asia is home to 60 percent of the world's population and 30 percent of the world's land. The Pacific Ocean, Indian Ocean, Atlantic Ocean, Arctic Ocean, Arabian Sea, Bay of Bengal, South China Sea, Yellow Sea, and the Bering Sea all border on Asia. Fascinating sites such as the Himalayas, the Gobi Desert, and the world's highest and lowest points on Earth, Mount Everest and the Dead Sea, are all to be found there. We will begin our explorations in the northernmost country on the continent.

Russia is a transcontinental country located in both Asia and Europe. The Ural Mountains naturally divide the country; the part of Russia east of the mountain range is in Asia, and the part west of the Urals is in Europe. But since over 60 percent of Russia is located in Asia, I am including it in my Asia section. Russia is the largest country in the world, so it has a very diverse culture. Russia is so large that it spans eleven different time zones! Also, it has the largest forest area of any country!

Russians love dark breads such as dark rye bread, and a family of four often eats three to four loaves per day! I find this fascinating! A typical day includes four meals. Again, fascinating! In the morning, usually it includes coffee; lunch is generally light, with maybe two courses. Dinner is the biggest meal of the day with four courses. Dinner starts with an appetizer like herring with vinegar or cheeses. The second course is a soup. The third course is meat and vegetables or potatoes. Dessert follows in the late evening at perhaps 9:00 or 10:00 p.m., with tea or coffee and something sweet like ice cream or cake.

BEEF STROGANOFF WITH BUTTERED NOODLES

INGREDIENTS:

1½ lbs. sirloin (sliced in 2" strips, ¼" thick)

2 Tbsp. butter

2 Tbsp. olive oil

½ cup onion (sliced thin)

1 carrot (thin sliced half rounds)

12 oz. button mushrooms (¼" slices)

1 Tbsp. Worcestershire sauce

2 cups beef stock

1½ Tbsp. cornstarch

3 Tbsp. water

½ cup half and half (for lower fat, substitute ½ cup dairy or soy yogurt)

2 tsp. fresh dill (optional)

Salt and pepper

Fresh parsley for garnish

4 cups egg noodles (cook according to package directions)

DIRECTIONS:

Prepare 4 cups og egg noodles according to instructions on package. Prepare all other ingredients as specified in the ingredients list. In a medium saucepan, stir-fry the sirloin in the butter and olive oil for 2-3 minutes or until meat is browned. Remove meat from pan. Add the onion, carrots, and mushrooms, and stir-fry for 3 minutes. Add the beef stock and Worcestershire sauce to the meat mixture and bring to a medium boil. Mix the water with the cornstarch and add to the pan; lower heat and simmer for 15 minutes. When the sauce has thickened, add the half and half and stir. Add the meat and the dill and heat through. Serve over noodles and garnish with parsley.

REMMI NOTES: This is a yummy stroganoff. It is quick and easy and qualifies as comfort food...but it is not American, it is truly Russian! Enjoy this scrumptious dish!

"When you have made as many mistakes as I have, then you can be as good as me."

—Wolfgang Puck

Traveling southwest from Russia, Tajikistan is one of the smallest countries in the world in terms of area, and its borders include Uzbekistan, China, and Afghanistan. Its natural resources include zinc, mercury, lead, silver, and gold. Much of the food in Tajikistan is influenced by the cuisine of nearby countries, like Russia, Afghanistan, and Kyrgyzstan, as well as foods introduced from Persian cuisine. Usually, Tajik meals start off sweeter and then move on to a soup and sometimes a meat of some type. Bread plays a key role in Tajik cuisine; some may even consider that it is not a meal without bread.

One fairly unique Tajik dish is Qurutob, which is a creamy, cheesy sauce served with a flaky pastry-like bread called "fatir." In Tajikistan, it is made with "qurut," a form of salty cheese, which is heated after mixing with water. Qurut is hard to find, but Greek yogurt serves as a similar substitute. Qurutob is a refreshing dish that is served on a communal plate. Occasionally meat is served with it; if so, it's usually lamb. It's a very simple and fun dish that many Tajik people think of as a national dish.

QURUTOB

INGREDIENTS:

1 sheet of frozen puff pastry (thawed/cut into triangles)

3 cups Greek yogurt

½ cup water

4 Tbsp. Parmesan cheese

1 tsp. salt

3 Tbsp. vegetable oil

1 medium onion (medium dice)

4 tomatoes (small dice)

4 green onions (thinly sliced at a slant)

¼ cup cilantro (chopped)

DIRECTIONS:

Prepare ingredients as specified in ingredients list. Place the puff pastry on a baking sheet and bake according to package instructions. Let it cool. Place the triangles on a large platter. In a medium saucepan, heat the yogurt, water, and Parmesan over medium-low heat. Remove from heat when just warmed. In a medium skillet, add oil and sauté onions over medium-high heat until translucent.

Place the yogurt in the center of a large platter and top with the sautéed onions and oil. Add the tomatoes, green onions, and cilantro. Serve with the puff pastry and enjoy!

REMMI NOTES: Qurutob is a much simpler dish to make than it is to pronounce. This dish is quite easy to assemble and customize. The recipe I provided is a simplified version, but you can also add meat to make it a fuller meal. I also used puff pastry as a substitute for "fatir," but there are recipes available if you want to make this dish closer to the original. In Tajikistan, they serve this on a large platter, and people eat from it with their hands, which can get a little messy but is very fun!

From Tajikistan, we travel southeast to the coastal nation of Israel in the Middle East. Israel shares borders with Lebanon, Jordan, Syria, and the Mediterranean Sea. Israel is a very interesting country with a rich history—it has more museums per capita than any other country in the world. It is home to the Dead Sea, location of the lowest place in elevation on the Earth! Israeli people consume the third most vegetables in the world. Israel's cuisine integrates many influences, including Jewish and Mediterranean cuisine.

A few popular dishes are falafel, hummus, couscous, and shakshouka, a tomato-based egg dish eaten at breakfast. Israeli cuisine is filled with olives, chickpeas, tomatoes, and eggplant—it incorporates a lot of fresh produce. Another staple of Israeli cuisine is pita bread, a pocket bread usually stuffed with salads, meats, or other snacks! Lunch is a very important meal, and a typical quick lunch is sabich or sabih, which is an Israeli sandwich of sorts served in pita bread, usually filled with eggplant, eggs, tahini sauce, hummus, and Israeli salad.

SABICH (ISRAELI SANDWICH)

Prep time: 20 minutes • Cook: 10 minutes

INGREDIENTS:

Israeli Salad Ingredients:
2 medium tomatoes
  (medium dice)
1 English cucumber
  (medium dice)
½ cup red onion
  (small dice)
1½ cups Italian parsley
  (finely chopped)
¼ cup extra virgin olive oil
¼ cup lemon juice
Salt and pepper to taste

Tahini Sauce Ingredients:
½ cup sesame seed paste
  (tahini paste)
½ cup warm water
1½ cloves garlic (minced)
2 Tbsp. lemon juice
1 Tbsp. parsley (minced)
Salt to taste

Sabich Ingredients:
¼ cup canola oil
1 eggplant (peeled and
  sliced in ½" rounds)
4 pita breads (cut in half to
  make half pockets)
3 eggs (hard-boiled and
  sliced crosswise)

DIRECTIONS:

Prepare ingredients as specified in ingredients lists. For the Tahini Sauce, combine all ingredients in a food processor or blender and purée until completely mixed. Set aside. For the Israeli Salad, mix together the tomato, cucumber, onion, and parsley in a medium bowl. Add the oil and lemon juice right before serving. Season with salt and pepper to taste and set aside. In a medium pan, add oil, turn heat to medium-high, and pan-fry eggplant slices until tender and golden on both sides, 2-3 minutes per side. Remove from the pan and let it sit on a paper towel to remove extra oil.

To assemble the sabich, put a few slices of eggplant in the pita pocket. Drizzle about 1-2 Tbsp. of tahini sauce to the pocket. Add the sliced eggs and spoon Israeli Salad in the pocket. Serve and enjoy!

REMMI NOTES: Researching Israel took me back to when I was younger and I met an Israeli chef named Itzik. He introduced me to common Israeli food, but more specifically to the kosher way of cooking that much of Israel follows. I thought it was interesting that, through the generations, they have kept the customs from scriptural texts written thousands and thousands of years ago. My favorite Israeli food is Israeli Salad. I love it so much, because it is so uniform, so simple, and very refreshing. Its only real dressing is olive oil and lemon juice, which really bind well to balance the acidity of the dish. The salad is a great addition to the Sabich, but it can work well as a stand-alone salad as well. Trust me, once you learn how to make Israeli Salad, you'll always have a go-to recipe when you're in a bind!

Southeast of Israel and surrounded by the Arabian Sea, the Indian Ocean, and the Bay of Bengal lies India. It is the world's largest democracy, with a population of 1.2 billion people. Chess and the number system were invented in India. Yoga, which has existed for over 5,000 years, also originated there. The national animal of India is the Bengal tiger, and the national flower is the lotus. India is home to the Taj Mahal, the white-ivory marbled mausoleum of renown. The world's largest gathering of people anywhere takes place in India at the Kumbh Mela Festival, celebrated over the course of twelve years. India has the world's lowest meat consumption per person. About 70 percent of all the world's spices come from India.

Like all food, Indian food has been influenced by various other civilizations. Indian food is different from any other in the world, both in taste and how the food is cooked. Since the cuisine is so diverse, Indian food is often divided by regions: north, south, east, and west, with each region producing different flavors and dishes special to India. Indian cuisine is known for its spiciness; so if you're like me and enjoy the heat, Indian food will be right up your alley. Biryani is a popular Indian rice-based dish; it is said that it originated during the Mughal Empire. It can be served with meat or vegetables, but it makes a great meal in itself.

CHICKEN BIRYANI (CHICKEN AND RICE)

INGREDIENTS:

2 cups basmati rice (soak in water 15 minutes)

¾ cup plain yogurt

1 tsp. cumin

4 tsp. garam masala (divided)

1 tsp. turmeric

1 tsp. chili powder

2 cloves garlic (minced)

2 Tbsp. lemon juice

Salt and pepper to taste

4 chicken legs and 4 chicken thighs (cut in half if large)

2 Tbsp. olive oil

1 large onion (sliced thin)

¼ tsp. crushed red pepper

5 cups water

½ tsp. saffron (mixed with ¼ cup water)

2 Tbsp. butter (mixed with saffron water)

1 large tomato (medium dice)

¼ cup almonds (sliced and toasted)

¼ cup mint (sliced)

¼ cup cilantro

1 lime (cut in 8 wedges)

DIRECTIONS:

Presoak the basmati rice in water for 15 minutes. Prepare all of the ingredients as directed. Combine the yogurt, cumin, 2 tsp. garam marsala, turmeric, chili powder, garlic, lemon juice, and salt and pepper to taste in medium bowl. Place the chicken in the yogurt marinade, coating the chicken on both sides. In a medium pan, add oil and fry the onions until golden, then add the crushed red pepper, remove from pan, and set aside. Add the remaining Tbsp. of olive oil to the pan and heat to medium. Add the chicken and discard marinade left in bowl. Sear on each side. Add a half cup of water to the pan, cover, and cook on medium-low for 15 minutes.

Meanwhile, prepare the rice by first draining and then adding it to a pan of boiling and salted water. Add the remaining 2 tsp. garam marsala. Cook the rice on high until it is almost done, with a slight crunch when tested (the rice will cook more when added to the chicken mixture). Drain rice and set aside. Scatter half of the fried onions and the tomatoes into the chicken pan. Spread the drained and partially cooked rice on top of the chicken mixture. To keep the rice fluffy, do not press down. Drizzle with the saffron and butter mixture. Place a piece of foil over the pan, cover with a lid, and cook on medium-low for 15 minutes until rice is tender. To serve, place the biryani on a large platter and garnish with the remaining fried onions and the almonds, mint, tomatoes, cilantro, and lime wedges. Serve the raita on the side.

INDIAN RAITA

INGREDIENTS:

1 cup plain yogurt

½ cup cucumber (seeded, small dice)

½ tsp. coriander

1 Tbsp. lime

Salt and pepper to taste

2 Tbsp. cilantro for garnish

DIRECTIONS:

Seed and dice the cucumber. In a medium bowl, mix all of the ingredients and garnish with cilantro. Serve with the Biryani.

REMMI NOTES: Although it takes a lot of preparation to gather all of the ingredients necessary for Biryani, it is worth it in the end. Biryani is a classic Indian dish that I always love to eat when I visit Indian restaurants. It was definitely a challenge to prepare it the first time, but what I learned is the importance of each step, especially with the rice. I know it sounds tedious to put foil over the pan and cover it with a lid, but this ensures that the steam is trapped and all of the flavors inside meld together to create a delicious dish. Plus, it is really important that you do not overcook the rice the first time you cook it. Since it is cooked again, you want it to be just al dente when you first cook it, so you don't end up with mush. But once you are on the final step, you'll realize that it's pretty rewarding to make such a complex dish, so give yourself a pat on the back! I tend to go light on spices, but if you can handle it, go ahead and add more.
Make sure you take the time to make the raita...it makes this great dish nothing less than fabulous!

From the north of India, we cross the border into east China. While writing this book, I was so excited to research China because, although I already knew a lot about it, I still learned so much! China has the biggest population on Earth, with over 1 billion people. Besides a lot of people, China also has many festivals. One of these festivals is the Spring Festival, the biggest festival of them all for Chinese people, which celebrates the beginning of the Lunar New Year. It is a fifteen-day celebration, which makes it the longest public holiday. They eat mustard greens as well as rice congee, my favorite Chinese dish! Another festival is the Moon Festival, or Mid-Autumn Festival, a harvest festival that celebrates people being together, giving thanks for blessings, and praying. One of its major traditions is to make and share mooncakes. Mooncakes are traditional Chinese pastries with sweet fillings of many flavors including red bean paste, lotus seed paste, chocolate, and green tea!

One of the main styles of cooking is Cantonese, which consists of stir-fried dishes. Rice is a major staple, which is why it is in so many dishes. Bean sprouts and cabbage are other staples of Chinese cuisine. Since they have so much access to vegetables, their dishes are usually filled with vegetables; and they do not eat a lot of meat, so they often use tofu as protein. These are just some of the reasons why vegetable fried rice is so common and popular!

CONGEE (RICE PORRIDGE)

Prep time: 15 minutes • Cook time: 1 hour

INGREDIENTS:

1 cup jasmine rice (rinsed and drained)

9+ cups water

Salt and pepper to taste

Green onion (sliced thin)

Soy sauce

DIRECTIONS:

Place the rice in a bowl and cover with water. Drain the rice. Repeat this step until the water is clear. Add the rice, water, and salt and pepper to taste to a medium stock pot. Bring to a boil, then lower to a simmer, stirring the rice every 15 minutes. Add more water if the mixture is too thick. The congee should be ready in 1 hour. Garnish with green onion and place soy sauce on the table.

REMMI NOTES: I know I describe things as "comfort food" frequently, but Congee is truly comfort food! It is often served at breakfast, and meats and vegetables can be added for a hearty stand-alone dish. When pairing with other more complex dishes, it is served very simply with a garnish or two to complement the other dishes.

CHINESE VEGETABLE FRIED RICE

INGREDIENTS:

2 Tbsp. vegetable oil

1 small onion (small dice)

1 carrot (peeled, small dice)

¼ cup red bell pepper (small dice)

2 green onions (sliced thinly)

2 cloves garlic (minced)

2 cups cooked white rice (day-old or leftover)

1 tsp. soy sauce

1 tsp. sesame oil

1 Tbsp. oyster sauce

1 large egg

½ cup frozen peas (thawed)

DIRECTIONS:

Prepare all of the ingredients as specified in the ingredients list. First, separate the cooked rice so that there are no clumps. Add a half Tbsp. of oil and the vegetables to a wok or large sauté pan. Stir-fry until the vegetables are well mixed and slightly tender (3-4 minutes). Push the vegetables to the side of the pan and add another Tbsp. of oil. Add the rice and stir until rice is lightly toasted. Mix the vegetables and rice in the pan until well combined. Add the soy sauce, sesame oil, and oyster sauce to the rice and stir until combined.

Push the rice to the side of the pan and add another half Tbsp. of oil. Add the egg into the open space in the pan with the oil, and use a spatula or spoon to scramble the egg into small pieces. Mix the rice with the egg. Add the peas to the pan and stir until well combined. Serve immediately and enjoy!

REMMI NOTES: One of the best things about a stir fry is that it is simple and quick to make! Also, for the cooked white rice, you can use leftovers from the night before. The key to this dish is the flavor, so when you add your sauces it is very important to taste the rice and adjust until you get the flavor that you like. Overall, this dish is a big hit in my home because my family loves to eat it and I love to make it, so I hope you and your family love it just as much!

Japan is an island nation in the Sea of Japan, roughly 1,900 miles east of China and just east of Korea. The Japanese love coffee, and they consume 85 percent of Jamaica's coffee production. Sumo is the national sport, but they love baseball as well, and it is the largest spectator sport. Roughly 70 percent of the country is made up of forests and mountains, so farming and residential development is limited. Japan is made up of roughly 6,800 islands.

Japanese people prefer fresh and seasonal foods. They live long lives since they eat a healthy diet. They eat more fish than any other country in the world; a total of 17 million tons is consumed each year. The Japanese are known for the artful and beautiful way they present food. Rice is served at every meal. Noodles are a big part of their diet, and it is considered most proper to make noise and slurp your noodles, as this gives the chef a sense of pride that you are enjoying your noodles.

JAPANESE RAMEN

INGREDIENTS:

3 Tbsp. olive oil (divided)

3 chicken breasts

2 tsp. ginger (minced)

⅓ cup soy sauce

¼ cup grape juice

8 cups chicken stock

1 cup mushrooms

Salt and pepper to taste

4 eggs

12 oz. ramen noodles

1 can canned corn (kernels, not creamed)

1 cup scallions (sliced on bias)

2 jalapeño peppers (sliced thin/
   seeds removed)

1½ cups bean sprouts

Extra soy sauce

Water and ice for preparation of eggs
   and ramen

DIRECTIONS:

In a medium pan, heat 2 Tbsp. of oil and sauté the chicken until golden brown on both sides and cooked through. Set aside until cool, and then slice thin. Heat the remaining 1 Tbsp. of oil in a medium stock pot, and when the oil is hot, add the ginger. Sauté for 2–3 minutes. Add the soy sauce, grape juice, chicken stock, and salt and pepper, and bring to boil. Reduce heat to simmer and add the mushrooms.

Boil water in a small pan, then add unshelled eggs to boiling water and simmer for 6 minutes. Place eggs in a bowl of water with ice for 5 minutes. Then peel the eggs, slice them in half, and set halves aside. Cook ramen noodles according to package directions. Drain, then divide into four warmed bowls. Add equal amounts of the hot stock with the mushrooms into the four ramen bowls. Top with the sliced chicken, corn, and scallions. Evenly divide the eggs onto the ramen bowls. Serve with jalapeño slices, bean sprouts, and additional soy sauce on the side.

REMMI NOTES: Ramen noodles are a Japanese staple! One of the best things about ramen is that you can customize the flavors and toppings to your liking. If you like a little heat, you should add Sriracha for a bolder spice factor! Typical toppings for ramen include pork, eggs, cabbage, and scallions. You can also add spinach and corn if you are more vegetable-inclined!

From Japan, we return to the mainland for our next destination. Known officially as the "Lao People's Democratic Republic," Laos is a thriving Asian country. It is surrounded by China, Myanmar, Vietnam, Cambodia, and Thailand. Its official tourism slogan is "Simply Beautiful" due to its many natural attractions, like the Kuang Si Falls and the Khone Phapheng Falls, which are the largest in Southeast Asia. Laos also has many festivals, the majority of which are focused on either religion or agricultural seasons. The Food and Agriculture Organization reported that 72 percent of its cultivated land is solely for rice. This is why rice is such an important part of the Lao diet, especially sticky rice. Actually, people in Laos eat more sticky rice per person annually than anywhere else in the world.

The green papaya salad originated in Laos, however, some version of this dish is served in every part of South Asia. This salad is usually served with sticky rice with some type of vegetable on the side to cool down the dish, as it is usually very spicy. The unripened papaya has a very tangy taste and crunchy texture.

GREEN PAPAYA SALAD (THAM MAK HOONG)

INGREDIENTS:

- 1 unripe green papaya (peeled and shredded)
- 1½ cups cherry tomatoes (halved)
- 1 Tbsp. soy sauce
- 1½ Tbsp. lime juice
- 1½ Tbsp. brown sugar
- 2 cloves garlic (minced)
- ¼–½ tsp. crushed red pepper
- ¼ cup fresh basil (chiffonade)
- 1 butter lettuce (washed, leaves separated)
- ¼ cup mint leaves (chiffonade)

DIRECTIONS:

Prepare all of the ingredients as specified in the ingredients list. Place the papaya and cherry tomatoes in a medium bowl. In a small bowl, mix the soy, lime juice, sugar, garlic, red pepper, and basil together. Salt and pepper to taste. Toss the papaya and tomatoes with the dressing just before serving. Garnish with mint. Serve with the butter lettuce as a wrap for the salad.

REMMI NOTES: This very famous salad is served with a variety of ingredients, including meats and fish. Fish sauce is one of the basic ingredients, but I substituted soy sauce here, as I like that flavor better. My reference for the salad suggests wrapping it in butter lettuce. Usually it is served with sticky rice that acts as the vessel for the salad. If you have a hard time finding green papaya in your grocery store, they are usually available in Asian markets. This salad is very refreshing. Love it!

Leaving Laos, we travel through Thailand to its southern border, where we encounter Malaysia, a very multicultural country with influences from China, India, Persia, and Britain. It borders on Thailand, Indonesia, and Brunei, and it's linked to Singapore. Its largest city is Kuala Lumpur, the capital. In Kuala Lumpur, there is the Central Market, which is a huge marketplace filled with shops of all sorts. Malaysia is rich in history; Hari Merdeka, or the National Day of Malaysia, is celebrated on August 31st. It is also one of seventeen biologically megadiverse countries on Earth and contains 20 percent of the world's animal species. Malaysia is also home to the world's tallest tropical tree—it is 262 feet in height and ten feet in diameter.

Their unofficial national dish is Nasi Lemak, a fragrant rice dish cooked in coconut milk and served in a banana leaf. It is usually served for breakfast. However, Chicken Curry is an unsung popular dish in Malaysia. It is different from Thai and Chinese curry and has its own unique flare! The curry paste is the key to this dish, and I prefer to make mine fresh.

Malaysia has probably the most extensive and most exotic fruits I have ever heard of. There are many Malay salads where they mix cucumbers with fruit. I have always loved this combination. The "Durian" is considered the "King of Fruits," however, it is banned in many places like hotels and airports because the smell is so offensive to foreigners. Don't worry, I couldn't get my hands on a Durian, so I made my salad with two of my beloved fruit favorites, mangos and watermelon.

KERABU (CUCUMBER FRUIT SALAD)

Prep time: 20 minutes

INGREDIENTS:

1 cucumber (sliced thin in 'half moon' rounds)

1-2 medium mangos (large dice)

2 cups watermelon (cubed, large dice)

¼ tsp. crushed red pepper

2 Tbsp. lime juice

1 Tbsp. olive oil

1 tsp. sugar

Salt and pepper to taste

DIRECTIONS:

Prepare the cucumber, mangos, and watermelon as specified in the ingredients list. In a medium bowl, mix all of the ingredients. Chill for an hour before serving.

REMMI NOTES: This is the perfect salad to go with the curry dish because it is so refreshing. This is such a simple salad to make! Be sure to experiment with different fruit combinations with the cucumber.

KARI AYAM (CHICKEN CURRY)

INGREDIENTS:

Spice Paste:
½ medium onion (small dice)
2 tsp. ginger (minced)
6 cloves garlic
2–3 Tbsp. curry
¼ cup water

Curry:
2 Tbsp. canola oil
2 tsp. lemon zest
1 lb. chicken breast (boneless/skinless,
    cut into 1" cubes)
2½ cups coconut milk
2 tsp. sugar
1 tsp. salt
1 cup chicken stock
1 large potato (peeled and cut into 1"
    cubes)
1½ cups rice (uncooked)

DIRECTIONS:

Prepare the onion, chicken, and potato as specified in the ingredients lists. In a blender or food processor, combine all of the spice paste ingredients. In a large sauté pan, add oil and the spice paste and stir over medium heat until aromatic, about 4 minutes. Add in the lemon zest and the chicken pieces and coat well with the spice paste, then add coconut milk, sugar, salt, chicken stock, and potatoes. Simmer covered for about 30 minutes over low heat.

While the curry is cooking, add 3 cups of water to another pan. Bring to a boil and then add 1½ cups of white rice. Turn the heat to low and let the rice cook for 15–20 minutes. Set aside when finished. Once chicken is fully cooked and potatoes are tender, turn off the heat. Serve curry over rice and enjoy!

REMMI NOTES: Since this dish is very spice-heavy, the balance of sweet, spicy, citrusy, and savory flavors is extremely important. When finishing making the dish, taste your curry! Add sugar if you'd like it sweeter, lime juice to make it more citrusy, and more coconut milk for a creamier texture. Chicken curry is a hearty dish that does not require a lot of preparation, so enjoy!

"You know, food is such—it's a hug for people."

—Rachael Ray

CONTINENT OF AUSTRALIA

"Cooking with kids is not just about ingredients, recipes, and cooking. It's about harnessing imagination, empowerment, and creativity."

—Guy Fieri

Due south from Malaysia is the continent of Australia, an island continent located in the Indian and Pacific Oceans. It is both a country and a continent and has 16,000 miles of coastline. The Great Barrier Reef, the largest reef in the world, is located there. Its large desert area is known as the "Outback." The country is multicultural and over 25 percent of the Australian population are immigrants. It is the home of the koala bear and the kangaroo.

Australia's cuisine is heavily tilted towards seafood, as it is one of the largest producers of abalone and rock lobster. Beef, pork, and mutton pies are popular street foods. Their famous sweet treat, "Lamingtons," is a sponge cake dipped in chocolate and covered in coconut. The iconic spread down under is "Vegemite," which is a vitamin-packed yeast spread that is used to flavor many of their dishes, and is also served on toast. The Granny Smith and Cripps Pink (a.k.a. Pink Lady) apple varieties originated in Australia.

AUSTRALIAN FAMILY FEAST

KUMARA SALAD

Prep time: 20 minutes • Cook time: 15 minutes

INGREDIENTS:

2 Tbsp. olive oil

2 medium sweet potatoes (peeled, ½"
   dice)

4 cups romaine lettuce (1" slices)

2 oranges (peeled and sectioned)

¼ cup green onion (sliced thin)

½ cup sour cream (low-fat)

1 Tbsp. vinegar (champagne or white)

1 Tbsp. orange juice

1 tsp. honey

1 tsp. lemon juice

Salt and pepper to taste

¼ cup roasted pistachios

Parsley (garnish)

DIRECTIONS:

Preheat the oven to 400 degrees. Prepare all of the ingredients as specified in the ingredients list. Put the sweet potato on a baking sheet and drizzle with the olive oil, then place in preheated oven for 15 minutes or until tender (taking care not to overcook). Remove from oven and allow to cool. Place lettuce leaves on a platter. In a medium bowl, mix the cooled sweet potatoes, oranges, and green onion. In a small bowl, mix the vinegar, orange juice, honey, lemon juice, and salt and pepper. Add the sour cream to the mixture and salt and pepper to taste. Mix the salad dressing with the potatoes and oranges and place mixture on top of the lettuces. Garnish with pistachios and parsley.

REMMI NOTES: I love sweet potatoes, and the kumara is well-loved in Australia. I love the flavors that come together with this dish...some sweetness, some saltiness, and overall deliciousness!

THE AUSSIE BURGER

Prep time: 15 minutes • Cook time: 15 minutes

INGREDIENTS:

1½ lbs. ground beef (formed into
    4 patties)
Salt and pepper to taste
4 pineapple slices (grilled)
1 cup canned pickled beets (drained)

4 eggs (fried soft)
4 pieces of butter lettuce
4 Tbsp. mayonnaise
¼ tsp. hot sauce
4 Kaiser rolls

DIRECTIONS:

Prepare the beef, beets, and eggs as specified in the ingredients list. On a heated grill, cook the hamburgers to desired doneness. Place the pineapple slices on the grill until grill marks are visible on both sides. Toast the rolls on the grill. Mix the hot sauce into the mayonnaise. To assemble, layer in the following order; bottom bun, hamburger, pineapple, beets, fried egg, lettuce, 1 Tbsp. hot mayo sauce, and top bun.

REMMI NOTES: I know this recipe isn't very complicated, but I just had to include it in this book because this burger is fantastic! When I have all of these ingredients…this is the burger that I make. You can add other ingredients like cheese, onions, and tomatoes, but beware, this is a tall burger already with all of the layered ingredients! Be sure not to overcook the egg, as you want all that gooey yolk to break on your first bite.

BEEF CURRY PUFFS WITH SPICY TOMATO CHUTNEY

Prep time: 25 minutes • Cook time: 40 minutes

INGREDIENTS:

Beef Curry Puffs:

2 frozen puff pastries (cut into fourths
   to create triangles)

2 Tbsp. olive oil

¼ cup onions (small dice)

¾ lbs. ground beef

1 potato (peeled, medium dice)

1-2 tsp. curry powder

2 tsp. Worcestershire sauce

Salt and pepper to taste

½ cup water

½ cup peas

2 Tbsp. milk

Spicy Tomato Chutney:

2 Tbsp. olive oil

½ cup onions (medium dice)

½ cup green pepper (medium dice)

2 cloves garlic (minced)

14 oz. can diced tomatoes

2 tsp. tomato paste

¼ t red pepper flakes

1 Tbsp. vinegar

1 Tbsp. honey

¼ tsp. cinnamon

Salt and pepper to taste

DIRECTIONS

Beef Curry Puffs: Prepare the vegetables as specified in the ingredients list. Preheat your oven to 375 degrees. Take the pastry from the freezer and cut each sheet into quarters. In a medium pan, sauté the onions in heated oil, then add the ground beef and cook until the meat is no longer pink. Add the potatoes, curry powder, Worcestershire sauce, water, and salt and pepper. Simmer for 20 minutes until the potatoes are (almost) tender. Add the peas and heat through. Place the puff pastry on a baking sheet. Divide the beef mixture on one-half of the pastry. Brush the exposed pastry edges with milk, fold to make a triangle, secure the edges with tines of a fork, and brush the top of the pastry with milk. Place in preheated oven for 15-20 minutes or until golden.

Spicy Tomato Chutney: Prepare the onions, green pepper, and garlic as specified in the ingredients list; then, in a small pan, sauté them in the heated oil for 2 minutes. Add the remaining ingredients and cook on medium-low for 20 minutes.

REMMI NOTES: The tomato chutney is worth the effort to serve with the beef curry puffs. Make sure you save any leftovers of this mouth-watering caramelized sauce and serve with crackers and hard cheese!

GRILLED PRAWNS WITH TOMATO LIME SALSA

Prep time: 20 minutes • Cook time: 5 minutes

INGREDIENTS:

12 to 16 large prawns (cleaned and halved lengthwise)

2 Tbsp. butter (melted)

2 Tbsp. olive oil

Salt and pepper to taste

2 large tomatoes

¼ tsp. red pepper

1½ tsp. lime juice

2 Tbsp. olive oil

Zest of 1 lime

1 lime (cut in wedges)

2 Tbsp. fresh mint (sliced)

DIRECTIONS:

Prepare ingredients as directed. Combine the melted butter with the olive oil and brush the prawns with the mixture. Add salt and pepper to taste. Place the prawns directly on the grill for 2 minutes shell side-down. Turn the prawns and grill 1 more minute. In small bowl combine the tomatoes, red pepper, lime juice, and olive oil. Place cooked prawns on a platter with the salsa, or serve in individual serving bowls. Garnish with the lime, zest, and fresh mint.

REMMI NOTES: Nothing else to say here but YUM!

TAKEAWAY MEAT PIES

INGREDIENTS:

4–5" pie tins
4 prepared pie pastries
2 Tbsp. olive oil
½ cup onion (small dice)
1 lbs. ground beef
½ cup carrots (small dice)
¼ cup celery (small dice)

¼ cup ketchup
¾ cup beef broth
1 Tbsp. cornstarch
1 Tbsp. water
½ cup peas
Salt and pepper to taste
Milk

DIRECTIONS:

Prepare ingredients as directed. In a medium pan, sauté the olive oil and onion in warmed oil for 1 minute. Add the ground beef and the carrots and celery. Cook until the meat is done. Drain any grease. Add the ketchup and broth and bring to medium heat. Mix the cornstarch with the water and add to the meat mixture. Cook for 15–20 minutes. Add the peas to the mixture and salt and pepper to taste. Using the pie tin to measure the rounds, cut 8 rounds of prepared pastry. Place one round in the bottom of each pie tin, evenly divide the meat mixture, and place one of the remaining rounds on each pie. Crimp the edges of the pastry to seal. Make a 1" slit in the top of each pastry to allow steam to release. Place pies on baking tray, and bake in oven at 375 degrees for 20 minutes or until the crust is golden. Serve with ketchup.

REMMI NOTES: Meat pies are considered the national dish of Australia. They are served by street vendors and are at most sporting and entertainment events. They're pretty simple to make and pretty delicious to eat!

COTTAGE PIE

INGREDIENTS:

Potato Topping:

2 lbs. Yukon Gold potatoes (unpeeled, medium dice; cooked)

½ cup sour cream (fat free)

½ cup chicken broth (fat free)

Salt and pepper to taste

Meat Filling:

2 Tbsp. olive oil

½ cup onions (small dice)

½ cup celery (medium dice)

2 carrots (medium dice)

1½ lbs. lean ground beef

¾ cup beef broth

1 Tbsp. tomato paste

1 cup frozen peas

Salt and pepper to taste

3 Tbsp. fresh parsley (chopped finely)

DIRECTIONS:

Preheat oven to 350 degrees. Prepare the potatoes as specified in the ingredients list. Mash the potatoes with the remaining potato filling ingredients and set aside. Add the oil, onions, celery, carrots, and meat to a medium pan. Cook on medium-low heat until meat is no longer pink. Drain any grease. Add the remaining ingredients except the parsley, and simmer until thickened. Place the pie ingredients in the bottom of a medium casserole dish. Spread the potato mixture over the pie. With the back of a medium spoon, sweep the potato up to form peaks. Bake for 20-30 minutes until warmed through. Remove from oven and garnish with parsley.

REMMI NOTES: My family has happily eaten versions of this beloved dish since long before we discovered it was an Australian classic! The base of onions, celery, and carrots is known as "mirepoix," a French culinary term. This dish is easy to whip up, since you cook almost everything at once!

PAVLOVA WITH KIWI AND BERRIES

Prep time: 30 minutes • Cook time: 1 hour

INGREDIENTS:

3 egg whites

1 cup sugar

¾ tsp. vanilla

¼ tsp. cream of tartar

1½ cup heavy whipping cream

Kiwi

Strawberries

Blueberries

Banana

DIRECTIONS:

Preheat oven to 250 degrees. In a medium mixing bowl, beat the egg whites until stiff using an electric mixer or by hand. Add the sugar ⅓ of a cup at a time, mixing in between additions. Add the vanilla and cream of tartar and mix until fully incorporated. On a baking sheet lined with parchment paper, place large scoops of egg white mixture in the middle, then form them into a roughly circular shape. Make a small depression in the middle, and create edges by pushing the egg white mixture from the middle outwards towards the sides. Bake for 50 minutes on the lowest oven rack, then allow to cool. While the Pavlova is baking, in another mixing bowl, whip the heavy whipping cream to make whipped cream. Store in the fridge until the egg white base is done baking. Place the meringue base on a platter. Spoon whipped cream into the center. Top with sliced kiwi, strawberries, bananas, and blueberries. Enjoy!

REMMI NOTES: The best thing about this traditional Australian dessert is that it is so adaptable! You can top with any combination of your favorite fruits or whatever may be in season! It's very light and easy to prepare! This dish is said to have been inspired by the famous Russian ballerina Anna Pavlova. Both Australia and New Zealand take credit for its invention, since she visited both countries!

"I tell a student that the most important class you can take is technique. A great chef is first a great technician. If you are a jeweler, or a surgeon, or a cook, you have to know the trade in your hand. You have to learn the process. You learn it through endless repetition until it belongs to you."

—Jacques Pepín

CONTINENT OF ANTARCTICA

Our final trek is south from Australia, where we come to the coldest place on earth. Antarctica is without a doubt one of the most unique and unusual continents in the world. The southernmost continent does not have many inhabitants other than its wildlife, including various kinds of penguins and seals. Despite the intensely cold climate, researchers from several countries have set up over thirty stations that run either seasonally or year-round! According to the Antarctica Treaty of 1959, which began with only twelve nations but now has fifty-three countries who have signed on, "Antarctica shall be used for peaceful purposes only;" this means that locations in Antarctica are primarily used to research various types of sciences, including astronomy, environmental science, biology, and many more!

During my research on Antarctica, I discovered a book entitled *The Antarctica Book of Cooking and Cleaning* in which co-authors Carol Devine and Wendy Trusler share their experiences from working in Antarctica during a cleanup project. The cleanup project was led by Carol, who has a passion for the planet and decided to lead a group of twenty-odd individuals to the frigid continent. Fortunately, I was able to talk with both authors and discuss not only their time in Antarctica, but most importantly, their food experiences. Contacting them has made this continent one of my favorites to research and write about. It is extremely fascinating to hear firsthand narratives about one of the most isolated areas anywhere. I hope you enjoy learning about it as much as I do.

INTERVIEW WITH WENDY TRUSLER

Carol mentions your desire for adventure as a factor in hiring you. When you first were contacted about the cleanup project, what were you thinking? Had you been to Antarctica before? What expectations, if any, did you set for the trip?

Antarctica wasn't really on my radar until a friend from the tree-planting world suggested I apply for the cook position on this project. I was intrigued by the adventure, and the nature of the cleanup project struck a chord with me, but it was timing as much as anything that propelled me to go.

For nine years I had balanced a life of food and art, cooking for tree-planting companies in the growing season, and pursuing my visual art practice for the remainder of the year. It was a good mix of creative pursuits, but since making the break from cooking in the bush the summer before, I'd been living somewhat precariously, so ironically for me work in Antarctica offered a much-needed degree of security.

The day Carol interviewed me, she showed me a map of King George Island hanging on the wall and pointed out all the different international bases. Within walking distance from Belllingshausen, the Russian base where we were to be stationed, was a Chilean, Uruguayan and Chinese base. I love austere landscapes and was excited about potentially living in such a remote setting, but my immediate thoughts were, WOW, If I get this job I'm going to learn so much. I set myself up to do so by challenging myself to collect recipes from as many different bases as I could.

Due to the scarcity of ingredients readily available of Antarctica, what, if anything, did you learn through improvising, whether it be about food or your own cooking abilities?

I have always espoused an "if I don't have it, I don't need it" cooking philosophy and was accustomed to improvising from my days cooking in remote sites across Canada. But in Antarctica the scarcity of some ingredients and abundance of others tested my creativity daily. That, coupled with remoteness in the extreme, forced me to embrace problems. All to say when I opened myself to adversity and cooking hurdles, I found I was able to strengthen my intuition and nurture a curiosity and playfulness in my cooking—elements I still find as essential as the right amount of salt.

You say that you grew up with imprecise descriptions for measurements and instead just learned measurements through

eyeballing or feeling or simply intuition. Do you encourage going by the book, or should people who cook (especially teens or kids) try to feel what seems right with ingredient measurements?

Oh, you are referring to my Mom's teasingly vague directives when I asked her "how much? how long?" cooking questions when I was a teenager. Although noncommittal, her replies—"about that much, until it's done"—made me feel for what I thought mattered and helped me develop opinions about the taste, texture, smell, and appearance of whatever I was making. I think the best cooking advice I can offer any cook is to find a way to dance between intuition and going by the book. Intuition is just another form of knowing, but that knowing can be strengthened with understanding and practice.

Take my chocolate chip cookies, for example: I loved baking as a kid and developed a feel for making chocolate chip cookies by first following the recipe on the back of the chocolate chip package. As I became more confident and competent, I started to experiment with the ingredient proportions and baking times. At the same time, I noticed the baking decisions other people made— how much flour, what kind of chips and how many, what kind of sugar—and tweaked my cookie recipe based on those observations. I made plenty of mistakes, but learned to trust my instincts along the way so that now when I bake, I can get the results I want by eyeballing and feeling my way through the ingredients.

In Antarctica, what was your best experience in the kitchen? Was it a time you had to improvise and discovered a new recipe? Was it cooking alongside someone else?

Please believe me, I'm not just fence-sitting when I say both examples you mention were best experiences. There is an amusing kind of flow I adore that comes with the challenge of cobbling together a meal or a dish from scant ingredients. In Antarctica, I pored over cookbooks trying to trigger ideas, and over narrow possibilities to come up with the most elegant solution possible, given the limitations imposed on a particular day.

Making ice cream to deal with an oversupply of both chocolate and cream for instance. I had never made ice cream and didn't think to bring an ice cream maker from Canada, and yet the playfulness of a frozen dessert on the frozen continent was much appreciated by all those who came for dinner that evening.

I deeply treasure the times when I was able to cook alongside others as well, especially when we didn't share a language and had to rely on drawings and gestures to communicate. By the time the ingredients and the method in the recipe were exchanged, we were friends.

Was there a specific type of cuisine or food that you tended to cook while in Antarctica? What were they?

Whether I was trying out something new or relying on my old standbys, I think my cooking is best described as comfort food with gourmet leanings. I liked to test the recipes I collected at the neighboring bases and loved the fluctuating sense of home that they brought to my cooking. Cazulea from Chile, Pollo Relleno from Uruguay, and Lena's Cabbage Pie were among my favorites.

How and where you serve a dish or meal is a key factor in making the ordinary extraordinary. Hands-on meals like "make your own pizza" night transform dinner into a conversation, which is helpful when dinner guests don't share a language. Another favorite was to surprise our volunteers by hiking to the worksite to serve them a cheese fondue lunch in a tiny refuge on the stone beach.

Provisioning for a trip to Antarctica seemed like a difficult task to manage, with the language barriers and cultural differences. What was it like to experience foods from different cultures that you had not tried before?

It is always an adventure to experience foods from different cultures, but what struck me most in our discussions and experiences in Antarctica were the similarities in cuisine, not the differences.

The evening I made pelmeni (the Russian answer to pierogies) for some of our Chilean neighbors underscores this. One of the Chilean officers commented that the half-moon shaped dough reminded him of empanadas. We talked about how many cultures fill pockets of dough with all manner of things. I added: pelmeni = pierogies = pasties = dumplings =

empanadas. The world became a larger and smaller place for all of us that night.

What tips would you give to young adults or teens who are interested in cooking but haven't yet started venturing into the kitchen?

This is an easy one, start with something you like to eat. Your first foray could be as simple as finding a creative new way to serve a dish that someone else has already made. It could be a way of presenting, cooking, or baking that you saw at a restaurant, on television, or in a magazine. Next, you could try to make it yourself.

Above all, like any good experiment, you must start with questions. Questions like what makes a dish taste, look, smell, and feel so good? Cooking becomes an adventure when you can notice the elements you like and discern how to enhance them through practice.

What was one of the best dishes you made in Antarctica? (You decide what "best" means—whether it was the easiest to make, the all-around favorite of those who ate it, or any other criteria you have in mind.)

For me, especially in Antarctica, best means how well a dish brings people together. My Honey Bread became an all-around favorite, both for its taste and for the way it helped our groups coalesce.

I typically served braids straight from the oven on the first night of every camp. You can't go wrong with warm bread no matter what. When you serve it, without a knife, to groups of people who don't know each other, it's transformative. Even the shy members of our teams were compelled to talk, lest they miss out on the bread.

I also love this recipe for its versatility. I use it to make my cinnamon bun, fruit nut rings, and as a base for pizzas.

What advice would you give for cooking meals with different cultural origins?

I always like to start by looking for the similarities between cultures in cooking so I can better understand the differences. The more you understand about a country's history, geography, climate, and economy, the more you'll appreciate the choices that are being made, which will help infuse your own cooking with authenticity.

What does cooking mean to you? Did the trip to Antarctica shape your thoughts about cooking in any way?

Cooking has always been a way that I ground and share myself. My awareness of this deepened in Antarctica, not so much in how it affected me personally, but more so in that I was able to see how my cooking grounded and brought others out of themselves. I don't face the same cooking challenges in my kitchen now, but I work to keep alive the curiosity, seat-of-the-pants resourcefulness, and generosity of spirit Antarctica infused me with.

In *The Antarctica Book of Cooking and Cleaning*, there are many incredible recipes—this super delicious and easy-to-make hors d'œuvre is one of them! The garlic shines in this dish, while the complementary herbs make for a fantastic combination. Straight from their book, Wendy and Carol present Roasted Garlic in Herbed Oil!

Inspired by Wendy's many creative dishes that her peers enjoyed in Antarctica, I decided to share some of my own recipes that are similar in ingredients or technique.

ROASTED GARLIC IN HERBED OIL

The inspiration for this dish was a four-foot-long double braid of Argentinean garlic that hung on the wall of my Antarctic kitchen. It is really more method than recipe, as much depends upon mood, pan size, and the herbs you have on hand. These proportions fit nicely into a small cast-iron skillet—feel free to ad lib with the herbs. I use fresh instead of dried when available, and once on a whim in Antarctica, I added a handful of the cranberries the Russians had given me. I like to keep them on hand at home now for the vibrant burst of color and unexpected flavor and texture they bring to this dish.

INGREDIENTS:

6 to 7 heads of garlic

Olive oil

1 tsp. coarse salt

½ tsp. peppercorns (try pink or green
   if available)

½ tsp. chili flakes

½ tsp. dried rosemary

½ tsp. sage

½ tsp. thyme

A few bay leaves

1 handful frozen cranberries

DIRECTIONS:

Preheat the oven to 350 degrees. Cut ¼" from the tops of the garlic heads to expose the cloves. Remove any messy bits of skin, but not so much as to compromise the bulbs' structural integrity. Place the garlic in a skillet or ovenproof dish. Having 5–6 arranged around the perimeter and one in the middle works well—leave a little space in between. Add enough olive oil to come up to ¼" of the side of the pan, and sprinkle with salt, peppercorns, and chili flakes. Turn the bulbs to coat with oil and reposition them cut side up.

To finish, tuck as many bay leaves as you think look nice between the bulbs, and then scatter the remaining herbs over top, crushing them between your fingers as you go to help release the flavors. Cover tightly with foil, and bake until the skins on the garlic bulbs are golden brown and the cloves are tender. This should take about 50 minutes, but check after 40 minutes and remove the foil to hasten browning if necessary. Add the cranberries 5 minutes before removing the baked garlic from the oven. You can roast the garlic ahead of time and add the cranberries when you are reheating it.

Serve tucked in beside warm braids of Honey Oatmeal Bread (recipe in *The Antarctica Book of Cooking and Cleaning*) or with other warm bread you have on hand. I like to encourage the use of hands to pull away and squeeze the cloves onto the bread, but I always have two small spoons at the ready for the less adventurous. A dish for the skins is a good idea. Makes enough for twenty.

WHITE BEAN BRUSCHETTA

Wendy prepared a White Bean and Roasted Garlic Pâté. She describes white beans as "noble" and exceptional for any occasion ranging from "tak[ing them] on an expedition" to "serv[ing them] at a cocktail party." With her high praise of white beans, I decided that White Bean Bruschetta would be a perfect dish that highlighted these legumes, utilized similarly as in Wendy's pâté.

INGREDIENTS:

1 baguette (½" slices)
2 Tbsp. olive oil
1 can of Great Northern beans (rinsed and drained)
Zest of half a lemon

Juice of 1½ lemons
1½ Tbsp. fresh basil (chiffonade)
1 Tbsp. olive oil
Salt and pepper to taste
Fresh parsley for garnish

DIRECTIONS:

Prepare the ingredients as specified in the ingredients list. Preheat oven to 375 degrees. Line a baking sheet with foil. On the baking sheet, arrange the baguette slices in a single layer. Using a brush or a spoon, lightly coat each slice with a touch of olive oil. Toast in the oven for about 10 minutes, turning crostini rounds around halfway through to make sure both sides cook evenly. Once toasted, set aside and let cool. In a bowl, add lemon zest, lemon juice, basil, and olive oil. Fold the beans into the sauce mixture. Place crostini rounds on a platter and spoon a Tbsp. of the mixture onto each round. Garnish with parsley.

REMMI NOTES: This is one of my favorite dishes because it is easy to quickly prepare and serve. The beans add a light heartiness while the lemon brightens up the whole dish! Be sure to keep an eye on the crostini while they are toasting to ensure that they are golden and crusty on both sides.

CABBAGE AND PASTA

Prep time: 20 minutes • Cook time: 15 minutes

Since Cabbage Pie was one of Wendy's favorite recipes from Antarctica, I knew I had to share a cabbage-centered dish as well. She explains that cabbage was a dependable food during her journey, and she has great "appreciation for [its] versatility." The cabbage pie she made was originally a family recipe shared by her Russian liaison. After reading this, I realized that my cabbage and pasta dish was very similar to her cabbage pie, because both recipes share the key ingredient—cabbage—and both are family recipes!

INGREDIENTS:

3 Tbsp. olive oil (divided)

½ cup bread crumbs (dried)

½ cup onion (small dice)

2 cloves garlic (minced)

¾ lb. penne pasta

6 cups savoy cabbage (sliced thin)

½ cup half and half (for lower fat, substitute ½ cup dairy or soy yogurt)

½ cup cooking water

Salt and pepper to taste

Zest of 1 lemon

1 lemon (sliced in 8 wedges)

¼ cup parsley (chopped)

DIRECTIONS:

In a medium pan, add 1½ Tbsp. olive oil and the breadcrumbs. Sauté the crumbs until golden, then remove from pan to cool. Add the remaining oil to the same pan and sauté the onions and garlic for 3 minutes. Prepare pasta according to package instructions, reserving ½ cup of cooking water when draining. Add cooking water to the onion and garlic mixture with the cabbage. Bring heat up to medium, then lower heat to low and cook for 3 minutes. Add the pasta and half and half to the pan and salt and pepper to taste. Divide pasta into four heated bowls. Garnish with the zest, breadcrumbs, parsley, and lemon wedges.

REMMI NOTES: At first glance, this dish seems a little wacky. Truth be told, it is a little weird, but in the best way possible. The cabbage gives the dish a nice hearty bite, while flavors of the onion and garlic combine well to create a savory taste.

SAVORY STUFFED ONIONS

Originally, Wendy crafted her baked stuffed onions because she had a superabundance of these versatile vegetables on hand. Due to her surplus of onions and dried apricots, she creatively developed her baked stuffed onions recipe, which included both ingredients. Though inspired by her sweeter version of stuffed onions, I decided that I would go for a more savory route.

INGREDIENTS:

4 medium onions (peeled)

Olive oil

4 oz. cream cheese (low fat)

¼ cup milk

Dash hot sauce (or more if you like it hot)

¼ cup parsley (chopped and divided)

Salt and pepper to taste

½ cup bacon (cooked and chopped)

½ cup panko

DIRECTIONS:

Prepare ingredients as specified in the ingredients list. Preheat oven to 425 degrees. Remove the top of the onion by slicing off a ½". Place the onions in a small baking pan and cook for 35 minutes. Remove the onions from the baking pan, and gently remove the inner core of the onion leaving a ½" shell. Roughly chop the inner core of the onion and set aside. In a small bowl, blend the cream cheese, milk, and hot sauce. Add the chopped onion, half of the parsley, and salt and pepper to the cheese mixture. Evenly divide the cheese mixture and fill each onion cavity. Evenly divide the bacon and top each onion, pressing slightly to settle the bacon into the cream cheese filling. Evenly divide the panko and layer on top of the bacon layer. Place onions back into the oven for 20 minutes until the panko is golden. Garnish with remaining parsley.

REMMI NOTES: I had never really tried to put onions in the spotlight in a dish, but this recipe certainly does! I loved the savory bits of bacon, which although tiny, boosted the flavor. The panko also added a contrasting and crunchy texture compared to the smooth filling.

CHICKEN WELLINGTON

Wendy recalls learning how to make Pollo Relleno, a dish that has influences from Uruguay, as a special meal. This dish is so fancy and complex it was usually served to foreign dignitaries. Imagine stuffing an entire chicken with sliced vegetables, other meats, and hard-boiled eggs. Similarly, this dish requires a stuffing of sorts. Chicken Wellington may be a little bit easier to prepare, but it is still qualified to serve to foreign dignitaries.

INGREDIENTS:

1 Tbsp. olive oil

½ cup onions (small dice)

4 oz. mushrooms (chopped finely)

¼ cup chicken broth

2 Tbsp. basil (chopped finely)

2 Tbsp. lemon juice

2 Tbsp. chives

2 cups half and half (for lower fat, substitute dairy or soy yogurt)

¼ cup cream cheese (low fat)

1 tsp. Dijon mustard

1 egg

1 Tbsp. water

1 package pastry sheet

½ cup red bell pepper (thinly sliced)

8 asparagus spears

4 chicken breasts (skinless, washed and patted dry)

Salt and pepper to taste

¼ cup parsley (chopped)

DIRECTIONS:

Prepare all of the ingredients as specified in the ingredients list. Preheat oven to 450 degrees. In a medium size skillet over medium-high heat add the olive oil. To make the duxelles, add the onions and sauté until the onions are soft. Add the mushrooms and the chicken broth. Simmer the mixture on medium heat for 8-10 minutes until it is reduced. Season with salt and pepper and set aside to cool.

To make the finishing sauce, combine the basil, lemon juice, chives, and salt and pepper with the half and half in a medium size skillet. Simmer until sauce is thickened.

To make the cream cheese sauce, in a small bowl, mix the cream cheese with the Dijon mustard, basil, chives, and lemon juice and set aside.

To prepare the Wellingtons on a lightly floured surface, roll the pastry sheet out to a ¼" thickness. Place the cream cheese mixture in the center of the pastry. Place the chicken breast (top side-down) on top of the cream cheese mixture. Cover the chicken breast with the 2 Tbsp. of the mushroom mixture (duxelles). Place a fourth of the red peppers, along with 2 spears of asparagus, on top. Then wrap the tower of chicken and vegetable in the pastry sheet. Fold one side over. Brush the top of it with the egg mixture. Fold over the other side of the pastry sheet and press it gently to make sure it is secure. Repeat procedure with the remaining two sides. Brush the completed pastry with the egg wash. Follow same procedure for remaining

Wellingtons. Place on greased baking sheet and bake for 40-45 minutes until pastry is golden brown. To serve, cover the bottom of a dinner plate with the sauce and place the Chicken Wellington on top. Garnish with parsley.

REMMI NOTES: Chicken Wellington is a classically elegant dish made simply. It is so easy to assemble once you have everything prepared, so make sure every piece is ready before putting the Wellingtons together! The chicken is so tender, and the cream cheese mixture is smooth with a whole lot of flavor. The red bell pepper sweetens the dish and the asparagus adds a crunchy texture—everything together in one convenient puff pastry is perfect!

BLUEBERRY GALETTE

I imagine that desserts were not Wendy's top priority in her Antarctic kitchen, but occasionally the provisions in abundant supply demanded them! She mentions making classic sweet treats, like chocolate cake, mousse, and even custard (which is difficult enough without being limited in one's food options). I usually do not produce many desserts at home, besides annual birthday cakes or holiday tarts. However, when I do bake, it's usually a fruit-based dessert like this Blueberry Galette!

INGREDIENTS:

2½ cups Blueberries

⅓ cup sugar

2 tsp. lemon zest

1 tsp. lemon juice

1 tsp. honey

1 Tbsp. cornstarch

1 package of frozen pie dough

1 egg

Pinch of sugar

DIRECTIONS:

Preheat oven to 400 degrees. In a medium bowl, mix together all ingredients except the egg. Place the pie dough unfolded on a baking sheet lined with parchment paper. In the center of the dough, add the blueberry mixture, leaving a 1" border of crust. Fold the edge of the dough around the blueberry mixture by making small pleats. In a small bowl, beat the egg and brush over outer crust. Sprinkle sugar on crust. Bake for about 25 minutes, or until crust is golden.

REMMI NOTES: Although, I don't make desserts very often, the Blueberry Galette is one of my favorites! It's a rustic-styled crust, so you don't need a pie pan, and you can shape it however you wish. The subtle notes of citrus from the lemon add a nice tang to this sweet dessert.

TURKEY CURRY SOUP

In Antarctica, it seems a bit expected to serve hot soup. Although Wendy did indeed craftily make other dishes, she also incorporated these generally broth-based dishes into the Antarctica diet. The origins of these soups ranged from leftovers of previous meals to a surplus of white beans (see bruschetta above). Regardless of the contents, soups are so versatile that you can whip up a quick, warm dinner using whatever you already have in your kitchen. This turkey curry soup relies on traditional kitchen staples, though a few ingredients may require a trip to the grocery store.

INGREDIENTS:

2 Tbsp. olive oil

1 medium onion (sliced)

1 celery stalk (¼" slices)

¼ cup flour

4 cups chicken broth (low sodium/ low fat)

2 carrots (½" slices)

2 cups turkey meat (cooked, medium dice)

1–14 oz. can diced tomatoes

2 tsp. curry powder

1 large apple (medium dice)

Salt and pepper to taste

¼ cup fresh parsley

DIRECTIONS:

Prepare ingredients as specified in the ingredients list. In a large pan, sauté onions and celery in olive oil for 3 minutes. Add the flour, then gradually add the chicken broth. Bring to a boil and then turn down to low heat and simmer. Add carrots, turkey, tomatoes, curry powder, apple, and salt and pepper. Simmer until the carrots are tender. Serve with parsley as a garnish.

REMMI NOTES: Soups are some of the easiest entrées to make, especially because there are so many! This Turkey Curry soup brings a variety of flavors into one bowl. Although it is a bit untraditional, this dish is perfect for providing comfort and warmth on any cold day.

POTATO SALAD

Wendy created a beautiful salad named "King George Island Salad"—just the name of it would make you want to eat it. The cornerstone ingredient of her great creation is a can of asparagus with additions of bacon and asparagus (very creative—can't go wrong with either). Wendy "became disheartened by the condition the lettuce arrived in after a long sea voyage, [and she] gave up on salad greens entirely and reached for [her] can opener." My Potato Salad has somewhat more limited ingredients, but the main constituent, the potato, has such a long shelf life that I imagine it is a staple in the coldest region in the world.

INGREDIENTS:

1½ lbs. Yukon Gold potatoes (washed and left whole)

4 eggs (hard-boiled and separated)

¾ cup green pepper (medium dice)

5 Tbsp. salad oil

3 Tbsp. red wine vinegar

⅓ cup green onion (sliced thin on bias)

Salt and pepper to taste

DIRECTIONS:

Prepare all of the ingredients as specified in the ingredients list. Boil potatoes until cooked, then run cold water over them to cool. In a medium salad bowl, mix the salad oil, red wine vinegar, and the egg yolks to form a paste-like sauce. Drain the potatoes and cut into a 1½" dice. Add the potatoes to the bowl. Roughly chop the boiled egg whites and add to the potatoes along with the green pepper and salt and pepper to taste. Gently mix the potatoes to coat with the sauce mixture and garnish with green onion. Note: If the sauce mixture is too dry, add equal parts of oil and vinegar and mix.

REMMI NOTES: This potato salad is ridiculously easy to prepare and is ready to eat straightaway. This dish may challenge your boiling abilities with the potatoes and the eggs, but it is an easy technique to master quickly. The combination of the soft texture of the potato and the crunch of the bell pepper, along with the tang of the red wine vinegar, makes this a nearly perfect salad dish.

INTERVIEW WITH CAROL DEVINE

Where does your passion for the environment stem from?

Hi Remmi. I grew up in Northern Ontario in Canada, where summers were short, magical bursts of blossoms and greenery, and in winter, nights were long, but we kids loved being in nature in all seasons. I feel lucky that I grew up in tight-knit communities and around cousins and neighbors, where we'd make snow forts and run around and play outside even when the sun had long gone to bed. I particularly love snow—maybe more after being further away from such intense winters, though Toronto has cold winters—because I'm concerned that glaciers everywhere are in retreat. That means less ice and snow and more water warming, and thus many health, ecological, and societal problems for us humans and other species. But now is a great time of opportunity too. We know the benefits of tackling overuse of natural resources and the benefits of tackling climate change. Today we have new technologies to use and ways to simplify our lives (walk, ride bikes, garden, and cook at home!) and help protect the environment now and for future generations.

What were you first thinking when you thought of the Antarctica trip?

Ha, great question. I was thinking I really want to go to Antarctica for a good reason. It was a deep desire. I loved that it was icy and cold, and marveled that it was a continent dedicated to peace and science in 1959, during the Cold War. Through a feat of collaboration of scientists and policy makers, the Antarctic Treaty was born and it was followed by an environmental protocol to protect this place of 'last wilderness' at the bottom of the world. With that inspiring history, and the fact that Antarctica was only relatively recently discovered and seen by humans—in the late 1800s, compared to other places where our human ancestors have been around for millions of years, I was drawn there. I found a way to go through leading this volunteer ecological cleanup pilot project—I found a path to my dream.

What were the biggest obstacles you first encountered in planning a trip to Antarctica?

One obstacle to overcome quickly was we needed volunteers for our cleanup project there! We had the idea, and we had the partners—a friendly company with icebreaker ships to take us volunteers there, and a Russian research station wanting our variably-skilled help with their cleanup—and we thankfully had Wendy (since our Russian partner insisted we bring our own cook), but we needed people to help do the project. Amazingly, when we advertised the opportunity, people were keen: individuals who devoted their vacation time to literally pick up trash. These wonderful volunteers from Canada, the U.S., Japan, the UK, and a few other countries signed up for this exploratory collaboration to put the spirit of the Antarctic Treaty into action.

You really rely on a hearty ship too. It's hard to get to Antarctica. Some very experienced sailors go there in sailboats, but you cross one of the harshest bodies in the world, the convergence of the colder Antarctic waters merging with the warmer sub-Antarctic waters. We were also lucky to travel on a Russian icebreaker with skilled expedition staff who took us to Bellingshausen, the research station, to do the cleaning work. Don't forget Antarctica is permanently uninhabited, researchers and research station staff only live there temporarily. Planning matters, and you have to bring what you need because it's an icy place with 90 percent of the world's ice and 70 percent of the world's fresh water, and long, long, cold, dark winters. We overcame obstacles related to food, materials, and logistics etc., but we had to think ahead and adapt as much along the way once we were in Antarctica too.

What advice would you give to teens who would like to make an impact on the world, whether it be through the environment or through other leadership projects?

I urge teens to do what you love and what has meaning to you. Follow your values and aim to work with and for people you respect. Respect yourself and know yourself foremost. What do you deep down wish to do, what are you good at or could get good at, what are your needs? Being able to work with diverse people and with people across disciplines will matter more and more. Get a great education, whether it's formal, experiential, or a combination of the two. And get work experience. And also, don't forget the importance of the life experience and inner strength you have gained from your families, your communities, and any challenges you've faced or overcome already, such as an illness, losing someone you love, or facing a big change you didn't expect.

Your generation will be important leaders. I urge you to be ethical, multi-skilled, collaborative-thinking, inclusive, innovative, and adaptable. I'm sure you will steward the planet and live with understanding of our interconnectedness and interdependence as humans across the world better than previous generations have. Communities are so important too, and we will continue to rely on them more in this era of climate warming and problem-solving. Be determined, creative, get yourself a bit out of your comfort zone, enjoy yourself, and let yourself seek your goals and even change your mind along the way. The line isn't straight always, and in the curves and bends you'll learn more, meet new collaborators (as I did in Wendy, luckily), find challenges, overcome them, and learn, see, and do new things.

Work in teams; this is good. No matter your age or what discipline you work in or what topic interests you, this is how change happens—together we make a wave, or refine ideas and make products, ideas, laws, or innovations better. When I got involved with leading the Antarctic cleanup expedition years ago with the Russian Antarctic Expedition, it only happened because there was collective interest in doing it, and because we had partnerships and other people who believed in it and had the will, the experience, and the different expertise to pull it off. We all took a risk working together on an unknown project, and it paid off in some surprising ways! It's a delight to share about our project with new audiences like young people through you. Lastly, don't forget that leadership is also helping others to find and use their voice and skills, not only being in front of the group, podium, or room.

What was your favorite memory of your trip in Antarctica? (Did this memory involve food?)

Now that you mention food, how could I not say how I loved how food brought us together in Antarctica—we were a group of people from many countries and cultures. Food is fundamental to life, and we think of it more consciously when we are in remote places or regions where food scarcity and security are serious issues—which is the case in too many parts of the world today. I remember a meal before Christmas in Antarctica just after our first volunteer cleanup team arrived to Bellingshausen, the Russian Research Station on the Antarctic peninsula where we were based.

Wendy had made her famous honey oatmeal bread, alongside a delicious meal (it's noted in the book). Hungry for dinner after orienting the new volunteers to the station, we Canadians

and Americans sat with our Russian hosts in a warm room on the top of a hill with the chilly Antarctic night wind blowing outside. (It was light still, in the Antarctic summer the sun barely sets.) Only a few Russians spoke some English other than Lena, our liaison officer. Wendy delivered two big warm braided loaves of bread. It smelled heavenly. There was no knife, but there was butter, and we were dying to dig in. Wendy was back in the little kitchen, I'm sure smiling, as we stared voraciously at the bread, unsure what to do. She came back in and said, "Break it with your hands." Wendy did a great thing, which was to help us overcome some awkward shyness and even language barriers through food. Once we broke pieces of bread together, we were physically and metaphorically connected. Food does that; sharing meals and doing new things together unifies us.

Another fond memory was eating Wendy's delicious food down there, far away at the bottom of the world where the Russians helped us set up a kitchen with food brought from Argentina. Lastly, how could I not mention the glorious glaciers we saw. They were these white, white, sometimes bluish, thick blankets, sometimes with black rock sticking out. They are moving rivers that have a lot to do with giving us people and animals water, water that along with food, air, sun and energy sustains our lives. The nature and wildlife in Antarctica are breathtaking. And the penguins, frankly, are adorable and really coordinated at climbing up rocks or snow, despite the odd way they walk.

ON ANTARCTICA

Antarctica will always be one of my favorite continents to learn about because of its slightly mysterious nature, even though its temperatures are freezing day and night. *The Antarctica Book of Cooking and Cleaning* and its co-authors, Wendy Trusler and Carole Devine, have taught me that you can always have a great time and a delicious meal when you have good company, regardless of where you are on the planet. These dishes are a combination of my personality and the different dishes that Wendy prepared and created in her time on the southernmost continent. I hope you enjoyed learning about their Arctic experiences and the recipes inspired by their adventures!

ACKNOWLEDGMENTS

Woo! You made it! How was your trip? Was it a little chilly in Antarctica? I figured it might be. I hope you have had an amazing journey, and that you don't need to buy any snow globes or key chains from a local gift shop, because now you have these dishes as gifts! Now, there are a few people that I need to thank for this grand adventure of a cookbook!

First and foremost, thank you for reading this cookbook! I truly hope your travels were delightful and that you had a fun time making healthy dishes!

Thank you to my amazing family. You all have been my rock during this process, and without your constant support (albeit, sometimes begrudgingly, but I probably deserved it), I would not have been able to accomplish this. A very special boatload of gratitude goes to my mother and business partner, Nancy Smith. I don't know how you put up with me sometimes, but I thank you for doing so. I love you all.

A huge thank you to Mango Publishing and everyone there for making this cookbook happen! Thank you to Brenda, Hannah, and Michelle especially, for ensuring that we stay on the right track along the way!

Thank you to my friends for keeping this a secret for a while and for always supporting me in my cooking endeavors. I promise that I will make you all food soon.

Thank you to all my business mentors, partners, and friends who have helped me become an entrepreneur and have taught me to always be determined and motivated. One single shout-out to Deedra Determan. You have continued to offer so many resources and have helped with so many business endeavors in the years I've known you! Also, many thanks to Wes Bergmann, BetaBlox founder, for your strong belief in me and pushing me to do the best.

Thank you to Wendy Trusler and Carol Devine, co-authors of *The Antarctica Book of Cooking and Cleaning*! You both made the Antarctica section truly shine! Our conversations have been a joy, and I loved reading about your adventures in Antarctica, as they inspired me greatly!

Thank you to everyone at Sodexo who has grown with me on my entrepreneurial and culinary adventures! A truly special thank you to Richard Hill and his wonderful marketing team.

Also, a special thanks goes to Chef Bill Harris for his patience and expertise on improving my culinary design skills.

Thank you to the Food Network for my opportunity on *Chopped*, which led to the making of this cookbook!

Arrivederci until next time,

Remmi

ABOUT THE CHEF

Remmington "Remmi" Smith is a nationally known speaker, author, and TV personality. As a teen entrepreneur, she is passionate about making a change to the childhood obesity epidemic and, linking the skill of cooking to improved nutrition, uses her influence to promote cooking education to build healthy lifestyles. She created the TV series *The Culinary Kid* and is the "Ambassador for Health and Wellness" for the international food service company Sodexo. In that capacity, her video series *Cook Time with Remmi* airs in over four thousand schools and is seen by an audience of 3.5 million. She also serves as a Junior Board Member for Independent Youth, an organization that promotes teen entrepreneurship.

Remmi has appeared on numerous TV shows, including the Food Network's *Chopped*, Harry Connick Jr.'s talk show, *Harry*, and *Business Rockstars*. She travels all over the United States and has made presentations to Congress, the National School Board Association, Facebook, Google, KidMetal, and various large family entertainment venues, among others.

She is the author of *Global Cooking for Kids*, a Gold Addy award-winning cookbook, and a regular contributor to edible magazine in Tulsa. She has been named a "Global Teen Leader" and the 2016 Ambassador for the Internationally recognized Three Dot Dash. The popular entrepreneur site Teen Business designated Remmi as one of the "Top 20 Entrepreneurs" and she has also been recognized as one of the "Top 20 to Watch" by the Foundation for Advancing Alcohol Responsibility, alongside Olympians, professional athletes, and members of Congress. The nonprofit organization Food Tank has recognized her as one of "20 Young People Changing the Food System"; additionally, Remmi was named on Food Tank's international list of "101 Innovators Changing the Food System."

She recently won the Inc. Magazine/Cox pitch contest which has led to the launch of her new service "Chef Club Box Fresh," a subscription meal kit delivered directly to your door. The aim of this service is to encourage teens and kids to acquire skills in cooking. Her salad dressing is sold at Whole Foods, Walmart.com, and several specialty stores; further, BetaBlox, a business accelerator and incubator, has recently signed her company to their program.

SOURCES

https://scholar.google.com/ (all countries)

muchmorocco.visitmorocco.com/ (Morocco)

caen-keepexploring.canada.travel (Canada)

https://www.playadelcarmen.org/mexico-travel-bureau/ (Mexico)

http://www.go2roatan.com/visit-mainland-honduras/ (Honduras)

http://www.visitcuba.com (Cuba)

www.experiencehaiti.org/ (Haiti)

http://www.visitjamaica.com (Jamaica)

https://sanjuanpuertorico.com/visitors-information-tourism-offices/ (Puerto Rico)

https://www.visitbarbados.org/ (Barbados)

http://www.tourism.gov.tt (Trinidad)

http://www.visitcolumbiamo.com (Colombia)

http://www.visitperu.com/visit-peruinfo/english/index.php (Peru)

http://www.spain.info/en_US/ (Spain)

http://www.egypt.travel (Egypt)

http://tanzaniatourism.go.tz/en (Tanzania)

http://www.malaysia.travel/en/us (Malaysia)

http://www.australia.com/en-us (Australia)

http://santiagotourist.com/sernatur-national-tourism-service/ (Chile)

http://santiagotourist.com/sernatur-national-tourism-service/ (Argentina)

http://www.inspiredbyiceland.com (Iceland)

http://www.visitfinland.com (Finland)

http://www.visitpoland.com (Poland)

http://turism.gov.md/index.php?l=en (Moldova, Greece, Mozambique, Tajikistan, Israel, and Laos)

Wendy Trusler and Carol Devine. Photograph by Sandy Nicholson. "Roasted Garlic and Herbed Oil," in *The Antarctica Book of Cooking and Cleaning* (New York: HarperCollins, 2015), 182. Reprinted by permission of HarperCollins.